W9-CNX-912

Gould

WORLD'S GREAT RACE DRIVERS

Exciting profiles of ten great race drivers in all classes of the sport—Indianapolis, stock cars, Grand Prix, sports cars, dragsters and more. Included are A. J. Foyt, Richard Petty, Jackie Stewart, Mario Andretti, Bruce McLaren, Don Garlits, Mark Donohue, Jimmy Clark, Parnelli Jones, and Bobby and Al Unser.

RANDOM
HOUSE
SPORTS
LIBRARY

illustrated with photographs

WORLD'S GREAT RACE DRIVERS

BY FRANK ORR

Random House New York

PICTURE CREDITS: American Hod Rod Association, 86 (left), 88–89, 95; Vernon J. Biever, end-paper; Alice Bixler, 2–3, 9, 32–33, 49, 76, 101, 105, 134; Central Press-Pictorial Parade, 55; National Hod Rod Association, 91; "Paris Match"-Pictorial Parade, 50–51; Pictorial Parade, 81; United Press International, 1, 6, 7, 8, 10, 13, 14, 21, 24, 36, 42, 53, 58, 60, 68, 83, 99, 112, 115, 118, 122, 124, 127, 129, 137, 140, 143, 147; Wide World, 16, 26, 29, 39, 47, 66, 73, 86 (right), 108.
Cover photo, SPORTS ILLUSTRATED photo by James Drake © Time Inc.

Copyright © 1972 by Random House, Inc.
All rights reserved under International and Pan-American Copyright Conventions. Published in the United States by Random House, Inc., New York, and simultaneously in Canada by Random House of Canada Limited, Toronto.
Library of Congress Cataloging in Publication Data
Orr, Frank. World's great race drivers.
(Random House sports library, 3)
SUMMARY: Profiles of eleven successful auto race drivers in all areas of the sport.
CONTENTS: Introduction.—A. J. Foyt.—Richard Petty. [etc.] 1. Automobile racing—Biography—Juvenile literature. [1. Automobile racing—Biography] I. Title.
GV1032.A1O7   796.7'2'0922 [920]   72-2038
ISBN 0-394-82416-4 ISBN 0-394-92416-9 (lib. bdg.)
Manufactured in the United States of America

Contents

Introduction   6

1. A. J. Foyt   11

2. Richard Petty   25

3. Jackie Stewart   38

4. Mario Andretti   56

5. Bruce McLaren   71

6. Don Garlits   85

7. Mark Donohue   97

8. Jimmy Clark   110

9. Parnelli Jones   123

10. Bobby and Al Unser   136

Index   149

Introduction

According to some polls, auto racing is watched annually by more spectators than any sport in the world. In the United States, paid admission totals for auto racing rank second only to horse racing (thoroughbred and standardbred combined). Each year, approximately fifty million spectators purchase tickets to motor sport events. They see races at the huge Indianapolis Motor Speedway, at the twisting Grand Prix road course at Watkins Glen, New York, and at local stock car tracks and drag strips in every corner of the country.

Racing cars come in many shapes and styles, and drivers compete for many different championships. Auto racing itself has literally hundreds of categories and classifications. Since this book contains profiles of drivers in many branches of racing, a reader may become confused unless he or she knows the major racing categories.

Let's start with the tracks on which the races are conducted. There are three basic types of tracks: ovals, road courses and drag strips.

Oval tracks are precisely that, a level circuit of asphalt (or dirt) where the cars race in a counterclockwise direction. They vary in length from the 2.5-mile "super-ovals" to the half- and quarter-mile local tracks. The cars make four lefthand turns around banked corners.

A road racing course duplicates the conditions a driver would encounter on regular roads. It contains corners of different angles in both directions and uphill and downhill sections. Road courses have no set length. The famed Nurburgring in West Germany is 14.2 miles long while Lime Rock Park in Connecticut is only 1.5 miles.

A drag strip is a straight stretch of paved road, one-quarter mile in length from the starting line to the finish with an additional stretch of track where the cars slow down after completing their runs.

There are four major classes of autos that compete on these tracks: open-wheeled cars, sports cars, stock cars and drag racing cars.

The open-wheeled cars have a single seat and an elongated, narrow body. No fenders cover the wheels and the driver is seated in an open cockpit.

The open-wheeled cars most familiar to U.S. racing fans are the championship cars of the U.S. Auto Club (USAC). These are the cars that compete in the Indianapolis 500-mile race each May and in other USAC-sponsored races. Frequently called "Indy cars," they are the largest of the open-wheeled racers and are powered by Ford or Offen-

hauser engines. They compete almost exclusively on oval courses. USAC also operates racing divisions for sprint and midget cars, which are smaller versions of the championship cars.

In the rest of the racing world, the most common open-wheeled racer is the "formula" car. Like the Indy car, it has a single seat, and an open cockpit. It is built to a rigid set of specifications or "formula" that governs weight and engine size.

The top formula car is the Formula 1, or Grand Prix car, in which drivers compete for the world driving championship. The Grand Prix races, staged

in many countries, are run on road courses. The Monaco Grand Prix is actually run through the streets of the city. The smaller-engined Formula 2 and 3 cars are raced mostly in Europe. Other formula cars include Formula A, Formula B, Formula-Ford, and Formula-Vee (Volkswagen), all of which are raced in the U.S. The Grand Prix races are governed by the International Automobile Federation, which also judges the competition for the world driving championship and organizes endurance races for auto manufacturers.

The sports car class includes production models

such as Triumphs and MG's which can be used as passenger cars and converted for racing. But the

best-known sports cars are the Group Seven cars which compete in the Canadian-American Challenge Cup Series. Group Seven cars must have two seats and covered wheels (fenders). Since there is no limit to the size of the engine in this class, Group Seven cars are the most powerful in the world. Sports cars generally compete on road courses, and so must be built to handle turns, hills and other road conditions. Sports car races are governed by the Sports Car Club of America (SCCA), which sponsors the Can-Am series, and the Trans-Am series for smaller "pony" cars.

The title "stock car" suggests that the cars in this class are similar to the average family sedan. They do carry the same basic body shape and the same names as the common passenger cars, but their engines are specially constructed, immensely powerful racing machines.

Stock car racing has divisions for all types of machines—from jalopies which have been rescued from the junkyard, to the top Grand National championship equipment. Stock cars are raced on oval tracks. The major sponsoring body is the National Associa-

tion of Stock Car Auto Racing, usually called NAS-CAR.

Drag racing classifications exist for almost every type of automobile powered by an internal combustion engine. The family car can compete in the lowest classifications, matched against a similar machine. Drag racing is a test of pure acceleration over the quarter-mile strip. The highest dragsters, the top fuel cars, are vehicles built only for acceleration. They may cost as much as $35,000 to construct. The major drag racing organizations are the National Hot Rod Association (NHRA) and the American Hot Rod Association (AHRA).

The organization of racing is so complicated that it sometimes confuses even the experts. But the most important people in auto racing are the drivers, and for many fans the drivers are the center of interest. Their skill and daring in this dangerous sport make them heroes to many and they deserve a place among the sports heroes of the world.

FRANK ORR

1

A. J. Foyt

Of all the auto races staged each year in all corners of the world, the two most famous are the Indianapolis 500 and the Le Mans 24-Hours of Endurance. Fame is about the only thing these two events share, however. The differences between the two races are immense.

The Indianapolis 500 is conducted on the 2.5-mile oval of the Indianapolis Motor Speedway on the Memorial Day holiday in late May. The cars are the open-wheeled, single-seat championship machinery sanctioned by the United States Auto Club (USAC). The cars make only four left-hand turns in $2\frac{1}{2}$ miles and the slightest rainfall causes the race to be halted.

The Le Mans race starts at 4 p.m. on the second Saturday of June. It runs through the night and the following day in almost any weather over a treacherous, irregular 8.3-mile course composed of public roads in the midwest of France. There are 20 turns. Many kinds of cars compete at the same time, ranging from big sports racers of the factory teams driven by top international stars, down to small touring sedans entered by amateurs.

Each of these races demands its own special kind of driver. But one man, A. J. Foyt, won the Indy 500 and the Le Mans in the same year, one of the most amazing feats in the history of auto racing. The two victories, which confirmed Foyt's standing among the greatest drivers of all time, were loaded with drama.

In 1967 the Indianapolis 500 was surrounded by more controversy than any race in its 56-year history. Andy Granatelli, the president of the STP Corporation, entered the revolutionary turbine-engined car, driven by Parnelli Jones, a long-time rival of Foyt. Drivers whose cars were powered by traditional internal combustion engines complained that the turbine engine should be banned from Indianapolis. Foyt made his objections loud and clear.

"I've always thought the Indianapolis Speedway is a proving ground for cars, not airplanes," Foyt said. "That jet car should be banned from the race. It's too expensive for most of us to compete with it and it has too big an edge in power on our engines."

Jones and his turbine-engined car quickly took the lead in the race on Memorial Day and had built a nine-second margin when rain halted the race. On the next day's restart, Jones regained control of the race again and piloted the turbine into a lead of 40 seconds. Driving a Coyote-Ford which he had built in his shop at Houston, Texas, Foyt held second place for most of the race, driving steadily and making no effort to catch Jones.

A. J. Foyt crosses the finish line in the 1967 Indy 500. The pole shows that his car, number 14, is in first place.

Then with three laps remaining in the race, the turbine car slowed suddenly on the backstretch and coasted toward the pits. A $6 ball bearing in the gearbox had failed. Foyt drove past Jones' crippled car, and into the lead.

"I was dead certain that the jet car was going to break," Foyt said. "I just knew it and I didn't try to chase him. I only worried about finishing."

When he headed around on his last lap, Foyt had

After the race, A.J. poses with his wife (left) and the race queen.

a premonition of danger ahead. Coming out of the fourth and final turn, five cars were involved in a wild, spinning crash.

"I don't know why, but I just had this instinct that there was going to be trouble before it was over," Foyt said. "I slowed down to about 100 miles per hour going down the backstretch. When I came around turn four and saw all the smoke and spinning cars, I couldn't believe it. I popped the car into low gear and pulled down to the inside of the track. When I saw where everyone was spinning, I just drove on through to the finish."

The victory marked the third time Foyt had won the Indianapolis 500. Only three other drivers— Louis Meyer, Mauri Rose and Wilbur Shaw—have accomplished this feat.

Two weeks later, Foyt was a member of the glamorous team of drivers entered by the U.S. Ford Motor Company at the Le Mans Endurance race. The Ford team was locked in competition with the Ferrari team of Italy. Ferrari had won the event for six consecutive years from 1960–1965. Then in 1966 Ford had swept the top three places in the top sports racer classification. The 1967 team from the Ford factory included five new Mark IV models in probably the most expensive racing lineup ever mounted for one race. The smaller Ferrari works fielded seven cars.

In the endurance test each car had two drivers who would alternate at the wheel. Foyt was teamed with Dan Gurney. Other Ford drivers included Mario Andretti, Lloyd Ruby and Roger McCluskey from the U.S. racing and international stars Bruce McLaren, Lucien Bianchi and Ronnie Bucknum.

At the start, Gurney moved into the lead. He set the fastest pace in Le Mans history. One or another of the Ford cars led the race all the way, and much of the time, the Foyt-Gurney duo was in front. Foyt's brilliant driving was something of a surprise. He seldom drove a road course and the popular opinion was that he was a great driver only on oval tracks.

"Many road racing people figured that Foyt was in over his head at Le Mans because of his limited sports car experience and the fact that he'd never raced at night before," said McLaren. "Well, after his first couple of stints in that Ford at Le Mans, no one mentioned again that Foyt was only an oval driver. His lap times were just as quick as Gurney's, or anyone else's, for that matter."

In the small hours of the morning, accidents and mechanical problems struck the Ford team with shocking suddenness. First, Andretti's car spun and was wrecked. McCluskey smashed his car into a wall to avoid hitting Andretti's machine. McLaren was forced into a long pit stop that dropped him out of contention and Bucknum's car was forced out of the race.

When almost ten hours remained in the race, Gurney and Foyt had to carry the Ford banner all alone. Although they had a five-lap lead, three Ferraris held second, third and fourth places, driving at an easy pace to take the victory if the leading Ford faltered.

From dawn to the 4 p.m. finish, however, the race belonged to Foyt and Gurney. When Foyt drove the bright red Ford across the finish line and accepted the checkered flag, the Foyt-Gurney car was more than four laps in front of the second-place Ferrari.

Foyt speeds across the finish line at Le Mans in 1967.

They had completed 388 laps, a total of 3,249 miles, at an average speed of 135.40 miles per hour.

His Le Mans victory was a crowning achievement in Foyt's racing career because it proved that he was as adept on the road courses as on the ovals of U.S. racing where he compiled an unequaled record. Had he moved into Grand Prix racing, Foyt might well have become world champion. However, the big Indianapolis machinery and late model stock cars were Foyt's first loves and in them he became the king of U.S. racing.

The cold figures of the record book reveal the Foyt greatness. He won the Indianapolis 500 three times (1961, 1964 and 1967). He was United States Auto Club national driving champion five times and won 43 championship races, both records. In the vanishing art of dirt-track racing, Foyt was the acknowledged master. He won the important Hoosier 100 dirt race six times. And he won 26 sprint car races and 20 events in the little USAC midgets.

He was USAC stock car champion in 1968 and runner-up in two other seasons, winning a total of 28 races. When Foyt ventured into stock car racing's toughest league, NASCAR, he won many important events including the Firecracker 400 at Daytona in 1964 and 1965, and two 500-mile NASCAR races in 1971.

Like many men in the front ranks of any competitive endeavor, Foyt burned for success and sacrificed many features of a normal life to attain it. From the time he launched his racing career in 1953 at the age of 18, driving jalopies on local Texas tracks, he wanted to run in only one place—at the front of the pack.

"The way I see it, the day you're happy with second or third place is the day you should get out of racing," Foyt said. "When you first get into racing, you're at the back of the pack and as you gain experience, you move up. When you've run at the front and won a few, there's no way you can sit back and be contented with second place. The day I don't want to be first is the day I'll quit."

Foyt was a perfectionist who learned every facet of racing from the ground up, including the construction and design of cars. He never asked his crew to do anything that he wasn't capable of doing himself.

Foyt was a mystery to many racing fans. He could be warm and approachable one minute, cool and aloof the next. His critics said he was arrogant, cocky, abrasive and unfeeling. His temper earned him almost as much publicity as his driving skill. He had no patience with crew members who failed to perform their jobs to the maximum and he fired mechanics on the spot for what he felt was "mechanical stupidity."

"If one of my crew members is fiddling around and not paying attention, then I don't want him around because it's my life he's fooling with," Foyt said. "When I get in that car, I don't want to risk getting hurt because of somebody's mistake. I watch every move a new man makes until he proves himself."

On the track, Foyt was no longer the hot-tempered man of the garage and pits. In the cockpit, he was a cool head. He appeared to take many chances, moving into places where lesser drivers wouldn't go. But his great ability to judge any situation and make the correct decision in a split-second was what separated him from ordinary drivers.

Although Foyt was not personally popular with the other drivers and made few close friends among them, the top drivers had great respect for his ability on the track.

"It's true that A.J. and I aren't friends, but we certainly aren't enemies," commented Mario Andretti, who had many tough racing battles with Foyt. "We're different personalities and we go our separate ways off the track. A.J. is a great race driver. If you are leading a race and he's in the field, you know that sooner or later he'll be nipping at you. You don't even think about it. You just know it.

"But you can race wheel to wheel all day with him and not worry. Like all of us, Foyt has had his bad moments, but most of the time, he lives by the rules."

Anthony Joseph Foyt, Jr., was born into a world of cars and racing in Houston, Texas, on January 16, 1935. His father was a former race driver who operated a garage and owned midget racers. A.J. picked up mechanical knowledge early in life.

When he was 17 Foyt quit school and started the long apprenticeship that was to carry him to the top. He raced motorcycles, jalopies and old stock cars on the dirt tracks of Texas where the competition was brutal and the timid quickly were weeded out. He graduated to midget and sprint cars, winning a large share of his races.

"People say I came up fast in racing but that wasn't quite true," Foyt said. "I started very young and built a lot of my own cars. I came right from the very bottom up and learned all the pitfalls of racing. It meant that nobody could put anything over on me because I knew what I could do."

When Foyt began to win consistently in midget racing, he attracted the attention of championship car owners. In 1957 he drove his first USAC big-car race. A year later he qualified for his first Indianapolis 500 and was running strongly until he spun on an oily section of track on lap 148 and was forced out of the race.

However, Foyt was approaching racing's top rank. He placed tenth at Indianapolis in 1959. His 1960 season started slowly and he had completed only 90 laps in the 500 when his clutch gave out. In September, he won his first championship race on the dirt track at Du Quoin, Illinois, and claimed his first USAC national title by winning three of the five remaining races in the season.

Foyt's first Indianapolis 500 win in 1961 was almost as dramatic as his 1967 victory. He took over first place from early leader Parnelli Jones and waged a lengthy battle with veterans Eddie Sachs and Rodger Ward. With ten laps to go, Foyt ran out of fuel and had to make a hectic pit stop during which Sachs moved into the lead.

Foyt charged back on the track in what appeared to be a hopeless chase of Sachs. But the drama was far from over. With only three laps remaining in the race and certain victory in his grasp, Sachs felt a strong vibration from the front of his car. One of his tires was worn almost through and he had to make a quick decision whether to pull into his pit for a

Foyt reaches for a cold drink as his mechanics attend to the car during the 1961 Indianapolis 500.

change or attempt to finish the race on the worn tire. He decided to pit and Foyt moved into the lead, winning the race by a mere eight seconds, the closest victory in Indy's history.

That first Indy victory placed Foyt's career in high gear and he continued to rule the USAC big-car circuit by winning the 1961 national championship. But the following season was a sour one for Foyt. In the Indy 500 a crew member failed to tighten a wheel properly during a pit-stop tire change and when Foyt had regained the lead in the race, the wheel came off. He spun wildly, but safely, into the infield and later fired most of his mechanical crew.

Foyt won five races to reclaim the 1963 national title but was forced to nurse an ailing car to a third-place finish at Indianapolis. That year he made his first venture into big league sports car racing and won the 252-mile Nassau Trophy Race in the Bahamas over a field of top international road racing stars.

In 1964 Foyt had the greatest season of any driver in the history of USAC's championship series. He won ten races, including one streak of seven consecutive victories, to sweep the national driving title. He claimed his second Indianapolis triumph in another hectic race in which two drivers were killed.

The lightweight, rear-engined Grand Prix style cars had been introduced at Indianapolis in 1961 and by 1964 several of them were in the field. Although the new machines were faster than many of the traditional roadsters, Indy veterans such as Foyt claimed the rear-engined cars were not safe and lacked the strength to stand up to the 500-mile grind.

On the second lap of the 500, sports car driver Dave McDonald, an Indy rookie, lost control of his rear-engined car. It smashed into the wall and burst into flames. Eddie Sachs smashed into the fiery wreck and both men were killed. Several other cars were wrecked and the race was halted until the track was cleared.

On the restart, Foyt stayed behind the rear-engined machines of Bobby Marshman and Jim Clark until, as he had predicted, they dropped out with mechanical problems. Indy then became a battle between the roadster veterans—Foyt, Parnelli Jones and Rodger Ward—and Foyt won by almost three miles.

"Many people said I was being backward when I claimed the rear-engined cars weren't safe," Foyt said. "Well, the new cars that came here from Europe first were very dangerous. I almost had bad accidents twice because of parts falling off them. They were put together like bicycles. When we started to build rear-engined cars, we made them into real race cars that were safe because they were well constructed."

In January 1965, Foyt had the only serious crash of his career in a stock car race at the Riverside road course in California. He was running at 140 miles per hour when two cars ahead of him slowed to enter a turn. When Foyt touched his brakes, nothing happened. To avoid hitting the cars, he tried to go around them. He slid off the track and bounced end-over-end down a 150-foot embankment. Rescue workers had to cut him out of his crumpled car. Foyt had broken bones in his back and heel and most of his body was bruised and scraped.

Three months after that accident, much of the time spent flat on his back in a cast, Foyt limped into Atlanta Raceway to run another stock car race. During the event, Foyt's throttle stuck and he scraped the wall, but brought the car to a safe stop. Later in the race, when leader Marvin Panch became ill, Foyt took over his car and won the race.

Although Foyt had become a wealthy man and had won just about everything worthwhile in U.S. racing, he laughed at predictions he would retire. His career continued with some good seasons and some bad. For instance, in 1966 he didn't win a major race and earned only $30,000 in prize money. A year later, he bounced back to win the Le Mans race, his third Indy 500 and his fifth national driving championship. In 1968, he won the USAC stock car title and was runner-up the next year.

His big ambition was a fourth victory at Indianapolis which would make him the all-time 500 king. He qualified for the pole position in 1969 but dropped out after 180 laps due to a loss of oil. In 1970 he had to nurse his car home to tenth place because of a failing gearbox and in 1971 he finished third.

He did win two major stock car races at Atlanta and Ontario, California, with brilliant driving performances.

Throughout his career, even after he became a super-star and could have entered only the major events, Foyt continued to appear at small races, where his name helped to sell tickets.

"Racing was very good to me and it has put me where I am today," Foyt said. "When I made it to the top I tried to repay the sport by running in smaller races as well as the big ones. I'll make the same effort if I'm running for a dollar as I will for $100,000. The day I just want to run in the big ones is the day I'll quit racing."

Looking for his fourth Indy victory, Foyt pulls onto the track in 1971.

2

Richard Petty

The late model stock cars roared around the Atlanta International Speedway in the 1971 Dixie 500 Grand National. The lead had changed hands 27 times in the first 297 laps. Then with 31 laps remaining in the race, leader Bobby Allison made a pit stop to add fuel to his 1969 Mercury.

When he roared back on the track, Allison trailed the bright blue 1971 Plymouth of Richard Petty by 2.1 seconds. The two stars of the National Association of Stock Car Auto Racing (NASCAR) were far in front of the other contenders, waging a furious battle for the $20,000 first prize money.

In the next eight laps Allison pulled even with Petty. The 25,000 spectators stood to watch the two masters of high speed oval racing make the big run for the checkered flag. Petty and Allison raced bumper-to-bumper and occasionally fender-to-fender, averaging 129 miles per hour with a top speed of more than 180 on Atlanta's long straights.

When they roared into a turn on lap 312, their cars touched and both machines almost went out of control as smoke rolled from the skidding tires. They were never more than a car length apart. Allison pulled even on the turns, then Petty regained the lead with his superior power on the straightaways. When the checkered flag fell on lap 328 to end the race, Petty was ahead by a mere five feet after 500 miles of brutally competitive racing.

For Richard Petty, collecting victory flags was an

The first man to win $1 million on the stock car circuit, Richard Petty holds up the trophy that put him over the top.

old story. He had won 134 Grand National races since he began racing in 1958 when he was 20 years old, but the Atlanta victory was especially significant. His winner's purse of $20,000 raised his career earnings to $1,017,853, making him the first driver in stock car racing history to top the magical $1,000,000 mark in prize money.

Petty accepted the prize money and the congratulations with typical modesty.

"A dozen years ago, I didn't even know about such a thing as a million dollars," Petty said. "I earned my first money when I was seven years old, about a dollar a day for picking tobacco. When I started racing, a million dollars was something I read about other folks having, but certainly not me. All I wanted was to make a living for my family."

Petty's racing kingdom was made up of the superovals and the small-town tracks in the southern United States. Petty was known to his legion of fans as "Richard the Lionhearted," and he reigned supreme. Stock car fans were working men and Petty raced in specially built, souped-up versions of the cars working men drove—Plymouth, Dodge, Ford, Mercury and Chevrolet. Stock car drivers often came from humble backgrounds. They were worlds apart from the sophisticated, often wealthy drivers of the European Grand Prix circuit.

Stock car racing had grown from a back-country pastime to a major spectator sport. And among the sport's growing number of fans, Petty was regarded as the greatest racing driver in the world.

"How can Jackie Stewart call himself the world driving champion," one Petty supporter snorted, "when he's never beaten Richard on a super-oval?"

Petty stuck to stock cars. He never ventured into the open-wheeled machinery of the Indianapolis circuit or the sports cars of the Can-Am racing on road courses. He turned down attractive offers from the U.S. Auto Club to drive Indy cars. He had entered and won stock car events staged on road courses, but he was famous for his mastery of the stock car ovals, which had their own kind of difficulty and danger.

"Open-wheeled racing cars never were big in the South," Petty explained. "Not even the midget racers could draw a crowd. I guess it's because people in the South are poor and those fancy race cars are so exotic that they don't know what to make of them. People can identify easily with stock cars. If a top driver is racing a Chevrolet, a lot of folks will come to see him because many of them drive Chevrolets.

"In stock cars, we do some real racing," Petty added. "Those Indy cars are so delicate that they can never touch each other without a lot of trouble. At the end of one of our stock car races, the cars are so banged up that we take all the sheet metal off and throw it away. It doesn't hurt the cars any and we really race each other."

Stock car racing blossomed in the South following World War II. One of the first kings of the stocks was Richard's father, Lee Petty, a hard-charging, tough driver who occasionally settled arguments with other drivers with his fists after the race. Lee Petty won 54 Grand National races, a record that was broken in 1967 by his son, Richard.

Following his retirement as a driver in 1962, Lee Petty became the top man in Petty Enterprises,

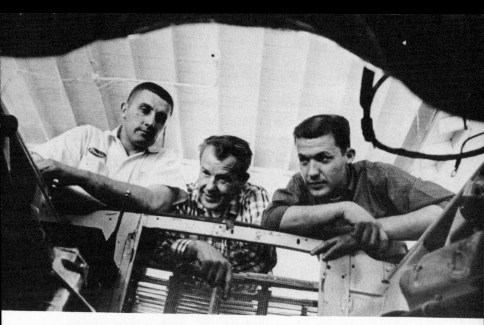

The Petty family, father Lee (center) and sons Maurice and Richard, look into an empty engine well.

which built and prepared the stock cars for Richard to race. The team's headquarters were in a large garage in Level Cross, North Carolina, a tiny village where half the population seemed to be named Petty.

The racing garage was surrounded by a barbed-wire fence to keep out intruders. Lee and his wife, Richard and his wife Lynda and three children, and his brother Maurice, who built the engines for the Petty cars, all lived in nearby houses. A cousin, Dale Inman, who masterminded the exceptional Petty pit crew lived just down the road.

Every day of the year, aided by friends and relatives, the Petty family worked on Richard's cars. These racing cars were like the passenger models whose names they carried only in basic shape. The Petty Plymouths were rebuilt from the ground up. Each piece of the car was made exceptionally strong to withstand hundreds of hours of high-speed racing.

Many top stock car drivers restricted their racing to the rich events on the super-ovals, competing in approximately a dozen races each year. Petty, however, averaged from 45 to 50 races each season, entering the super-oval competition and a long list of lesser events on small tracks in small towns throughout the South. At these small races, Petty was a big drawing card, but the purses for the drivers were small.

"We run our racing operation like a business," Petty said. "That means we enter every race we can. Some of the good boys only run the big ones, but our approach is to run 'em all. It's one way to keep sharp and also make money. I don't know anything about all the glory and glamor of auto racing. It's my business, the way I make my living, and we run it that way. If I could make more money running a service station, then I'd run a service station.

"We aren't much different than anyone else. We work eight or nine hours, five or six days a week. I prepare the chassis and drive the cars. Maurice builds and prepares the engines. My mother keeps the books and my father keeps track of all of us. I've found more hard work than glory in being a winning stock car driver."

Born in 1937, Richard was an excellent lineman in high school football. But as he grew up, his father was at the height of his racing career and Richard never thought much about doing anything except racing. He worked on his father's cars for several years. Then, in 1958, two races were scheduled for the same night. When his father entered one of them, Richard asked to drive a second Petty car in the other race. His father prepared one of the older cars and Richard competed on a half-mile dirt track in Columbia, South Carolina, where he finished sixth.

That launched Richard's driving career. He had many advantages over other young drivers. While they were forced to scratch for cars and money to stay in the sport, Richard had his father's cars and repair facilities. He also had the benefit of his father's long experience in stock car racing. Still, the early years were hardly glamorous.

"I didn't win anything in the first couple of years," Petty said. "I spent a lot of my father's money in racing cars. But he never said anything about it. He just let me find my own way in the sport."

Lee and Richard frequently raced against each other during the early years of his career. In one race at Atlanta, Richard was declared the winner by a slim margin over his father. Lee, however, charged around the track for an additional lap, then demanded a recount of the lap charts. When a check revealed that the race officials had stopped the race one lap too soon, Richard had to turn the trophy and the prize money over to his father.

From his father Richard learned the flatout professional approach to everything in racing—building, preparing and driving the car. Lee Petty's racing career began in a time when stock car racing was a gritty small-town pastime. He drove slow, poorly prepared cars over unsafe local tracks. There were few safety precautions and stock car racing offered very little money. The big stars were men such as Fireball Roberts, Joe Weatherly, Junior Johnson and Curtis Turner. Some of them had learned their driving techniques by transporting illicit moonshine whisky at night over the back roads of the South. From the beginning Lee Petty viewed stock car racing as a business and he taught Richard the same approach.

"I never saw many heroes in this sport," Lee Petty once said. "I've seen drivers with all the money, some with some of it and some with none. There were times when I was getting started in racing

when we hardly had enough money to buy the gro-
ceries.''

When Lee Petty retired as a driver in 1962, Richard was well on his way towards the top. He won his
first Grand National race in 1960 and finished second in the point standings that year with top-five
finishes in 16 of 40 races. In 1963, he won 14 races,
many of them on small tracks, and again was runner-up for the title.

His first super-speedway victory came in the 1964
Daytona 500. He won eight other races that year,
finished in the top five 37 times in 61 events and col-

Petty (#43) rounds a turn in the Daytona 500, on the way to his first super-
speedway victory in 1964.

lected $98,000 in prize money. He also won his first NASCAR championship.

The 1965 season was a bad one for Petty. NAS-CAR outlawed the big engines used in the Chrysler Grand National cars like the ones Petty drove. The company withdrew from racing and Petty pulled out, too. He tried drag racing briefly, but when Chrysler re-entered racing late in the season, Petty was back in action.

Petty's 1967 season was perhaps the greatest ever for a racing driver in any branch of the sport. Until that year, no NASCAR driver had won more than 18 races in a season. Then Petty counted 27 victories in 48 races, including ten wins in succession. He passed his father's career record of 54 wins, won three super-oval races, placed in the top five in 38 of 48 events, and collected $130,275 in prize money. He breezed to his second Grand National championship and confirmed his reputation as the best stock car racer in history.

Much of Petty's success was based on the clocklike teamwork of his racing organization. Although he always ran at high speeds, he almost always finished his races. This was testimony to the splendid preparation of the cars in the Level Cross garage. Under Dale Inman's leadership, the Petty pit crew was also extremely fast during a race, which was important because long stock car races often were decided in the pits. In a 500-mile race Petty often made seven pit stops for fuel and tires, but his crew seldom wasted a precious moment.

"Many teams use complicated signals between the driver and the pit crew," Inman said. "But we've been together so long that we have everything simplified. If Richard holds his nose, I know the engine is overheating. When he points over his shoulder, he wants to know who's behind and how far, and I can tell him on the pitboard.

"When he needs a tire, he points to the wheel before the car stops rolling. If it's suspension adjustment, he signals by pushing his left hand out as he passes the pits. Swinging the heel of his hand to the left means the car is pushing the front end. A swing to the right means it's too loose in the rear. That way we have some idea of what suspension changes are needed."

When Petty stopped in the pits, he watched only Inman, who gave him the "wait" signal by holding out his hand, palm down.

"I don't care if the crew pushes the car or beats on the roof," Petty said. "Until I get the 'thumbs up' signal from Dale, I don't move the car an inch."

On the big ovals or small tracks, Petty continued to win consistently. In 1969, he switched from Plymouth to Ford cars, and won ten races. The following season, he returned to Plymouth and the bright blue No. 43 again became the terror of NASCAR. Although a severe shoulder injury from a crash at Darlington Speedway sidelined him for a month, he won 18 races in 40 starts. That year, the Petty team fielded a car for young Pete Hamilton, who won the Daytona 500 and several other races on the NASCAR circuit.

Petty smashed several records during the 1971 season when he collected 20 victories in 40 races, passed the $1,000,000 figure in career winnings and

Petty's car flies through the air and lands upside down after he hit a wall in the 1970 Rebel 400 race. He received only minor injuries.

won a record season total of about $280,000. He also won his third NASCAR Grand National title. Only Lee Petty and David Pearson had won three titles.

The secret of the Petty success?

"Because I am involved in my cars through every phase of the construction and preparation, I think I know my machinery better than the drivers who aren't involved so much," he said. "I have real good equipment and I'm able to sort it out quickly.

"A driver must have ability, but there's a lot of instinct in it, too. The good drivers just know when to pass and when not to, when to charge and when to hang back, and most important, how much their car can take on that day on that track. You know how far you can push the car, but if you push it beyond that, you aren't going to accomplish much."

3

Jackie Stewart

Just before the start of the 1971 Canadian Grand Prix a steady drizzle began to fall at Mosport Park. The world's best racing drivers were worried. They hoped that the weather would clear and the sun would dry the track, or that the rain would fall in torrents.

"Drizzle is the worst possible thing," said Jackie Stewart, the jaunty little Scot who had clinched his second world driving championship earlier in the season. "You see, there is considerable oil on this track, and now it is wet. Either one is a problem by itself; together, they'll make it very slippery. A downpour would wash off the oil. But we can't do much about it. We'll just have to get on with it."

Stewart watched his crew put rain tires on his low-slung, bright blue Tyrrell-Ford Formula 1 car. Then he pulled a fireproof balaclava hood over his shoulder-length hair and covered the hood with his crash helmet, which was decorated with a band of the Stewart clan tartan. He squirmed down into the cramped cockpit of the Tyrrell and drove out on the twisting course. The world champion was ready to do what he could do best: drive a sophisticated, sensitive Formula 1 racing car.

Jackie Stewart in car 11 takes the lead at the start of the 1971 Canadian Grand Prix.

The 45,000 spectators huddled under umbrellas and bits of plastic sheeting as the 22 cars went through a warm-up lap. Two cars spun into the guardrail even at the moderate warm-up speed, showing again that the track was treacherous in the drizzle.

The cars stopped on the mock grid in starting formation. Stewart sat in the pole position, a place he earned with a record-shattering qualifying run the previous day. He glanced to his left through his rain-splattered goggles at Jo Siffert, second fastest qualifier in his British Racing Motors car, and Francois Cevert, also driving a Tyrrell, who shared the front row.

The field moved forward to the starting grid and paused briefly before the green flag was dropped by the starter. Stewart carefully fed the power to his wide Goodyear rain tires. As he moved into the first turn, he was in front of the pack, a rooster-tail of spray rising from his wheels.

At the end of the first lap around the 2.46-mile, ten-turn circuit, Stewart was in front by 200 yards. Ronnie Peterson of Sweden, one of the bright young drivers eager to challenge the champion, had knifed through the pack in his March 711-Ford from a seventh place starting position to second spot.

As Stewart predicted, the rain and oil on the track had made it nearly as slick as ice. Any extra power on a turn or the most minute oversteer sent cars into sideways drifts or spins.

"It was, beyond any doubt, the most slippery track I ever drove on," Stewart said.

Despite the conditions and Stewart's skill as a rain driver, Peterson closed the gap between his red March and Stewart's Tyrrell. Soon he was only a few yards behind, just far enough back to avoid the spray from the champion's wheels.

On lap 18 Stewart got trapped behind a slow car. Peterson shot ahead and quickly built a lead of 50 yards before Stewart got around the slower car.

Stewart stayed close behind Peterson. In lap 28, the margin between the two cars was only a few feet. When the young Swede spun on a corner, Stewart took the lead again. This time he refused to give it up. When the race was halted because of fog after 64 of the scheduled 80 laps, Stewart's was ahead by 39 seconds. He won $14,000, and his masterful performance under the worst possible conditions proved again that he was the world's best Formula 1 driver.

While most drivers stayed in the very slippery "groove" (the normal line around the track), Stewart had changed his pattern of driving to improve his traction.

"I worked on the gritty parts of the track much of the way around, breaking away from the normal line which was very treacherous with oil and water," he explained. "In the dry, the gritty parts would have been the same as driving on ball bearings. But, in the wet, the stones and gravel on top of the asphalt gave me better traction and adhesion."

The win brought Stewart's career total to 18 Grand Prix victories since he joined the Formula 1 circuit in 1965. His close friend and fellow Scotsman, Jimmy Clark, had set the record of 25 Grand Prix wins before he died in a 1968 crash.

Only about 15 men in the world are considered good enough to drive Formula 1 cars. When Stewart won six of 12 races in 1969 on his way to his first world title, he moved into the very front ranks of this select group. From 1969 on, the word in Grand Prix racing was: "If Stewart's car doesn't break, he'll win."

Stewart's accomplishments made him an international celebrity, and his business sense made him a very wealthy man. He lived in a 13-room mansion near Geneva, Switzerland, with his wife, Helen, and their two sons, Paul and Mark. But his hectic schedule didn't give him a chance to spend much time at home. In 1971 he traveled nearly 450,000 miles to make racing dates and personal appearances.

As a member of the Grand Prix Drivers' Association safety committee, Stewart also worked for higher safety standards, both for drivers and spectators. He made safety a personal crusade, leading driver boycotts of race tracks he considered too hazardous.

"I know it's unbelievable that we should be forced to have a strong driver protest before tracks will make improvements, but something had to be done to reduce the risk of injuries and death that race drivers face," he said. "We drivers shouldn't have to die because the proper safety barriers weren't installed, or burn in a fire because of insufficient firefighting equipment.

John Young Stewart was born in Dumbarton, a small town near Glasgow, Scotland, in 1939. His grandfather was head gamekeeper on the estate of a wealthy industrialist; his father, Bob Stewart, owned an auto repair garage in Dumbarton. From them,

Sporty Jackie Stewart after winning a 1971 Can-Am race.

Jackie acquired his two major interests—guns and cars.

"I was well drilled in the art and etiquette of shooting by my father and grandfather," Stewart recalled. "I started shooting rabbits and grouse whenever I had the chance. There was a clay pigeon trap on the estate and I would buy clay pigeons and shoot at them. By the time I was 14, I could hit ten of ten. On New Year's Day when I was 14, I won the first shooting competition I ever entered."

Stewart was exposed to auto racing at an early age when his brother Jim, eight years older than Jackie, began to race his car in local sports car events. Jim landed a place on Ecurie Ecosse, the well-known Scottish racing team. Later he drove for the Aston Martin factory team. But Jim permanently injured his arm in a series of accidents and retired in 1955.

"I traveled to the races with Jimmy and I lost interest in school," Jackie said. "Our garage was doing a great deal of sports car tuning and Jimmy was involved in that. When I was 15, I quit school and began an apprenticeship as an auto mechanic in my father's garage."

Stewart was a member of the 1955 Scottish clay pigeon shooting team and a year later he scored his first major victory in the West of England championship. By 1960 he was shooting for Great Britain and swept the British, Irish, Scottish, and the European and Mediterranean titles.

On his 21st birthday he participated in the trials for the British team for the 1960 Olympic Games at Rome. There he encountered what he calls "the biggest disappointment in my life." He had a rare off-day, missing eight of 25 targets, and failed to make the team.

By this time, Jackie was in charge of the motor-tuning side of the family business, working on high-performance cars. He went to night school and completed his apprenticeship as a mechanic. He attended races as a crew member on a friend's car, but he turned down an offer to drive. His brother's accidents and injuries had upset their mother and affected her health. Jackie knew that another driver in the family would upset her again.

But Jackie seemed destined for racing. Another friend, Bob McIntyre, wanted to drive a car on a race track to see if he had any ability. He and Jackie borrowed an AC-Bristol sports car and took it to the Oulton Park track for a test.

"Bob drove it a bit and I took it around a few times," Jackie recalled. "It was my first time in a good car at speed on a circuit and I really liked it, especially when I went faster than the lap record for that class of car."

To avoid worrying his mother, Stewart entered his early races under the pseudonym "A. N. Other," driving a variety of sports cars and winning many of the events he entered. In 1963, when he drove an E-type Jaguar to two victories at Rufforth, England, Ecurie Ecosse offered him a place on the team. Jackie dropped his disguise and accepted the opportunity.

In the well-prepared cars of Ecurie Ecosse, Stewart's great natural ability was evident quickly. In 1963 he entered 23 races and won 14 of them, setting several course records in the process.

"Anyone could see immediately that he was very good," said Colin Chapman, builder of the famous Lotus racing cars. "He had consistency and the correct attitude. And he could learn a course very quickly—and remember it."

Stewart soon met Ken Tyrrell, a lumber dealer with a passion for auto racing, who operated a team of Cooper Formula 3 cars. In March 1964, Tyrrell arranged for Stewart to drive a Cooper in a test at the Goodwood track in England. It was the first time the young Scot ever had driven a single-seat racer.

"I wasn't sure if I wanted to drive a single-seater but Jim Clark, who was well established in racing then and a sort of adviser to me, told me that I had to get into formula cars if I was serious about racing," Stewart said.

"Just going down to Goodwood was very thrilling. Bruce McLaren, who was almost like a god to me, had set up the car and I went faster in it than he did, which was something very difficult for me to believe."

Stewart drove the Cooper cars for Tyrrell that year and dominated the Formula 3 class, losing only two events. He soon was accepting offers from other teams and by the end of the year he entered 53 races and won 28 of them. Near the end of the season he drove a Lotus in the South African Grand Prix, winning the first heat before his car broke in the second.

His performance in Formula 3 cars did not go unnoticed. Three of the top Formula 1 teams offered him rides on the Grand Prix circuit for the 1965 season. The jump from Formula 3 to the bigger Formula 1 cars was a big one, so Stewart studied the offers carefully. He finally signed a contract with British Racing Motors (BRM).

"I wanted to join a team where I could develop at my own pace," Stewart said. "Graham Hill was BRM's number one driver and I knew I could learn a great deal from him."

Stewart scored his first Formula 1 Grand Prix victory in 1965 by winning the Italian G.P. at Monza. In 1966 he won the Monaco G.P., the most difficult race in the series because the course runs through the streets of the tiny principality.

In 1966 Stewart also appeared for the first time in the Indianapolis 500, driving a Lola owned by Texas oil millionaire John Mecom, Jr. Driving on the oval at Indy was a big change from the Grand Prix courses, but Stewart set out to master still another kind of racing.

Stewart's rear-engined Lola, based on the design of the small, quick Grand Prix racers, was still controversial at Indy. Large, cumbersome front-engined roadsters were still favored by the regulars. In 1965 Jimmy Clark had won the 500 in a rear-engined car, causing much resentment among American drivers.

Although he and his car were both "outsiders," Stewart quickly became the most popular driver in Gasoline Alley. During the month of testing, qualifying and racing, Stewart earned much favorable publicity with his frank, witty interviews.

In the race itself Stewart survived the colossal first-corner crash that wiped out 11 of the 33 starters, and was among the race leaders from the start.

He took over first place on lap 152 of the 200-lap race when the leader, Lloyd Ruby of Texas, was flagged off the track because his car had developed an oil leak.

Stewart moved to a commanding lead and appeared to have racing's richest purse in his grasp. But on lap 192, less than 25 miles from victory lane, Stewart's Lola lost its oil pressure and he was forced out of the race. When he pushed the car down the pit lane towards the garage area, the huge crowd gave him a standing ovation.

"It would be a shocking experience for anyone, but it was especially traumatic for a Scotsman," said Stewart. "A very shattering thing, indeed, for a Scot to be that close to $160,000 in prize money and not collect it."

Two weeks later Stewart had his first serious crash during the Belgian Grand Prix at the 8.7-mile Spa-Francorchamps course. Rain was threatening as the race started and when the field was four miles from

Stewart passes fellow Scot Jimmy Clark in the 1966 Indy 500. His car broke down eight laps from the finish.

the starting line on "Masta Straight," the cars encountered a sudden heavy rain squall.

Seven cars spun off the track and were wrecked. Stewart's BRM went out of control at 150 miles per hour. He spun several times and hurtled off the track back end first. The car slammed into a brick wall, then fell nine feet onto a concrete driveway.

Trapped in a pool of gasoline from the ruptured tanks, Stewart was pinned in the car by the crushed body. Drivers Graham Hill and Bob Bondurant, who had also crashed, worked for 35 minutes to free Stewart from the wreckage, using a wrench borrowed from a spectator. They had to work with extreme caution because any spark would have ignited the gasoline.

Stewart had minor internal injuries and his skin was scalded by the gasoline, which contained chemical additives. It took 45 minutes from the time he went off the road for an ambulance to arrive. This long delay, which might have been fatal, was what caused Stewart to mount his safety campaign. One of his special concerns was improving medical facilities on Grand Prix courses.

The 1967 Grand Prix season was almost a complete loss for Stewart with the BRM team. Plagued by engine problems, he finished only two of eleven races, earning a second in the Belgian G.P. and a third in the French race to finish in ninth place in the final driver standings.

In 1968 the huge French industrial concern, Engins Matra, decided to enter Formula 1 racing. Ken Tyrrell had entered the Matra Formula 2 cars for several years and Stewart had driven them with great success. Stewart quickly accepted Tyrrell's invitation to drive the new Matra Formula 1 car, which was powered by British-built Cosworth-Ford V-8 engines.

Success didn't come immediately. Stewart broke his wrist in a Formula 2 race, which hampered his driving for two months. At first the Matra F.1 car suffered from handling problems, but the excellent Tyrrell crew had solved many of them after the first three races.

Stewart was soon involved in a hectic scramble with Graham Hill and Denis Hulme of New Zealand for the world title. Stewart won the Dutch and German Grands Prix and then scored a convincing

Driving the new Matra, Stewart is on his way to victory in the 1968 U.S. Grand Prix at Watkins Glen, New York.

triumph in the U.S. Grand Prix at Watkins Glen, where he lapped everyone except Hill. Going into the final race of the season, the Mexican G.P., Stewart had 36 points, Hill had 39 and Hulme, in third place, had 33.

In the early laps of the race at Mexico City, Hill's Lotus and Stewart's Matra battled furiously for first place. Hill led for the first six laps with Stewart only a few feet behind. Then Stewart took over first place for three laps before Hill re-passed him.

Although Stewart was unable to regain the lead, he stayed on Hill's tail-pipe until lap 39 when his hopes for a victory and his first world championship ended. Stewart's engine developed a slight hesitation caused by "fuel starvation." A blockage in the fuel

lines prevented the normal flow of gasoline from the fuel tank to the engine.

As the fuel-feed problem worsened, Stewart fell far behind Hill. He finished seventh while Hill claimed an easy victory and the world title.

In 1969 Stewart and Tyrrell returned with an improved Matra and dominated the Formula 1 season. Not since Jim Clark won seven races in 1963 had any driver dominated the series the way Stewart did in 1969. The Matra was by far the most reliable car in the series, and with the brilliant work of the Tyrrell crew behind him, Stewart won six of eleven races and was in first place on 384 of the 807 laps in the series.

Stewart (foreground) poses with his full team in 1969.

Stewart opened the season with impressive victories in the South African and Spanish races before a broken drive shaft sidelined the Matra at Monaco. He built an overwhelming lead in the point standings with consecutive victories in the Dutch, French and British Grands Prix, then finished second in Germany to Jackie Ickx of Belgium.

Stewart won his sixth race of the season with a masterful drive in the Italian G.P. at Monza and, with three races to go in the series, he appeared to have a strong chance of equaling Clark's record of seven wins in a season.

In the Canadian Grand Prix at Mosport, Stewart jumped into the lead at the start, closely pursued by Ickx. During the first 32 laps of the race they ran only a few feet apart as Ickx repeatedly tried to pass Stewart.

On lap 33, Ickx attempted to move ahead of Stewart between the first two turns at Mosport, a short stretch where passing is very difficult. He was forced to drop two wheels off the pavement onto the graveled shoulder, causing his car to swerve into Stewart's. Stewart's Matra went spinning off the track but Ickx managed to keep control of his car and stay in the race. Damage to Stewart's car wasn't severe, but he was unable to re-start it because sand had gotten into the throttle slides. Ickx went on to win the race.

Bad luck continued to haunt Stewart and his car. His engine failed halfway through the U.S. Grand Prix, and poor tire adhesion contributed to a fourth-place finish in Mexico. Still, Jackie had won six G.P.'s in one year, no small accomplishment.

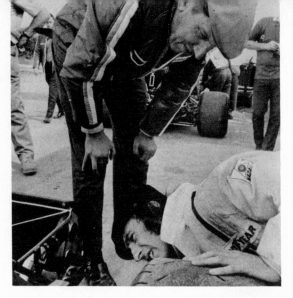

Stewart and his team manager Ken Tyrrell check their Tyrrell-Ford before a race.

For the 1970 season, the Tyrrell team switched to a new car, built by March Engineering, a British firm. The March cars operated impressively early in the season. Stewart finished third at South Africa and won in Spain. But the cars' performance deteriorated as the season progressed and Stewart's only other high finish was a second place in the Dutch G.P. Five wins in six races by Jochen Rindt earned him the world championship. Rindt died in a crash while practicing for the Italian G.P., even before the season was over.

In the final three races of the season in Canada, the U.S. and Mexico, Stewart drove a car which was actually built by the Tyrrell team in the garage at Tyrrell's lumberyard. The new Tyrrell failed to finish any of the three races, but when the car operated at peak efficiency, Stewart was usually ahead of the pack.

The three 1970 races allowed the Tyrrell team to test and refine the new car. When the 1971 season opened, Stewart and the Tyrrell were ready to pursue his second world championship. Jackie's teammate, young Francois Cevert of France, was starting what promised to be a brilliant Grand Prix driving career.

Following a second-place finish to American star Mario Andretti in the opening race in South Africa, Stewart won five of the next six races (Spain, Monaco, France, Great Britain and Germany) to clinch the world title with four races remaining in the series. His victory in the Canadian G.P. was his sixth of the season.

He was leading the U.S. Grand Prix, which would have been his seventh victory of the year, equaling Jim Clark's record, when a suspension problem slowed him down. Again he had to be satisfied with six wins instead of seven.

In 1971 Stewart also competed in the Canadian-American Challenge Cup series for big Group 7 sports cars. That series had been dominated by Team McLaren and its top driver, Denis Hulme. Stewart drove a Lola-Chevrolet and stirred up a great deal of interest in the series. But the car was new and untested and Stewart won only two races.

How does Stewart view the dangerous, demanding sport that has made him an international celebrity?

"There are times when I think it's a stupid sport," he explained. "I draw a great deal of personal pleasure from doing it, but when things go wrong, I really do think it's stupid. But those little spells don't last very long. Driving a race car is the most satisfying thing I've ever done and I hope I can continue to do it for another ten years.

"The challenge in auto racing comes from trying to synchronize the human element with the mechanical element, to mesh the driver's limit with the car's limit. Very few drivers in the world can accomplish this and that's why they're great.

"Racing has allowed me to provide the best possible life for my family, to travel places and meet people, things that I couldn't have done in any other field. I like what I'm doing and I guess that's the best reason I can give for why I'm a race driver."

Stewart (left rear) in the 1970 Race of Champions.

4

Mario Andretti

In 1969 the bright red, wedge-shaped Lotus racing car was called "the finest machine" ever to appear at the Indianapolis Motor Speedway. Mario Andretti was confident that this was the machine to end his years of frustration in the world's richest auto race.

Andretti had crashed the front ranks of Indy competitors with a third-place finish as a rookie in 1965. He seemed sure to be an Indy winner, but in the following three years he had nothing but bad luck. In 1966 his engine failed on lap 27. In 1967 his car lost a wheel on lap 58. In the 1968 race his engine quit after only two laps. He took over teammate Larry Dickson's car and its engine quit on lap 24.

Then in 1969 Andretti joined the STP Oil Treatment team, masterminded by Andy Granatelli, one of U.S. racing's great personalities. The red STP wedge racer had been designed by Colin Chapman of England, who built the famed Lotus cars for Grand Prix racing.

"It was a beautiful car," Andretti said. "For the first few days after it arrived at the track, I just wanted to stand around and look at it. I thought to myself that if I was ever going to win the 500, it would be in this car."

Starting a practice session in early May, Andretti took two slow laps in the Lotus to test the car's handling. The second time around, he increased his speed steadily down the back-straight in preparation for his first "hot" lap, and sped through turn three. There was a short stretch leading to the fourth turn which would bring him back to the main straightaway.

"When I headed the car into turn four, I heard a 'whirring' noise, which is a very bad sound because it means something is breaking loose from the car," Andretti said. "When the car spun around, I saw a wheel bouncing in the air and I knew I was riding on three wheels only. I hit the wall backward and the car started to come apart.

"Just as I hit the wall, I felt intense heat because the car was on fire. I covered my face with my hand and unbuckled the shoulder harness with the other. I could feel the heat through my driving suit, but around my face it was unbearable. I managed to jump clear before the car stopped moving."

The car was reduced to a pile of twisted junk. Andretti escaped with burns on his face. He would still be able to drive in the 500, but the beautiful Lotus was wrecked. Granatelli wanted him to drive one of the spare Lotus cars, but Andretti decided to drive a year-old car, the Hawk, which had been built by his crew chief, Clint Brawner.

Despite an engine overheating problem, Andretti was the second fastest qualifier in the Hawk, averaging 169.851 miles per hour in his trial lap. In an

Bad luck plagues Mario Andretti at Indianapolis. Above, his car loses a wheel in the 1967 race. Below, his new Lotus-Ford goes to pieces in practice for the 1969 contest.

effort to solve the overheating problem, the crew installed a second radiator in the Hawk. At first the Indianapolis technical committee ruled that the extra radiator was legal, but then they reconsidered and ordered it removed from the car.

"That ruling was a real kick in the teeth," Andretti said. "I really figured the extra radiator was my only hope of finishing the race."

Andretti's engine temperature soared in the early part of the race, but he brought it back to a safe level by dropping the engine revolutions. He squeezed ahead of top qualifier A. J. Foyt and held the lead for five laps until a spray of water hit him in the face. He thought a leak had developed in the radiator and he slowed down, allowing Foyt to take over first place. But Andretti soon realized that the liquid came from a drinking bottle in the cockpit. The bottle had tipped over, splashing him with a soft drink.

Andretti yielded second place to Roger McCluskey and, along with leader Foyt, they ran close together for 40 laps. Then McCluskey ran out of fuel and dropped back in the pack. Lloyd Ruby, who also had a long string of bad fortune at Indy, charged through the field into second place when Andretti and Foyt made their first pit stops.

When the turbo-charger on Foyt's engine malfunctioned, Indy's two "hard-luck" guys, Ruby and Andretti, were on top of the field. On lap 85 Andretti charged to the front. Then on lap 104 Mario logged a 40-second pit stop for fuel. Ruby grabbed the lead and held it during his pit stop.

On that day, all the good fortune rode with Andretti. On lap 106, Ruby made a routine pit stop for fuel and pulled away before his crew disconnected the hose from the car. The fuel tank fitting was ripped off the car and the popular Texan was out of the race.

That gave Andretti and his Hawk a one-lap lead on the field, which allowed him to run below the car's limits and not risk overheating the engine.

During the final 90 laps, he drove carefully and kept the lead to the end.

When Andretti drove into victory lane, Granatelli swamped him in a bearhug and gave him a much-photographed kiss on the cheek. It was Granatelli's first 500 victory after 24 years of trying both as a driver and an owner. Andretti had been trying for four years himself.

Defying his bad luck, Andretti roars home first in the 1969 Indy 500 and gets a kiss from Andy Granatelli (inset).

In a few short years Andretti had come to be rated the finest racing driver ever produced in the U.S. Certainly, he was the most versatile. He had earned victories in every form of racing—the championship, sprint and midget classes of the U.S. Auto Club, late-model stock cars on both road courses and super-ovals, and long-distance sports car racing.

Just a year before his Indianapolis victory, Mario cracked the ranks of the world's best drivers in Formula 1 racing. He shocked Grand Prix fans by earning the pole position on his first try in the 1968 U.S. Grand Prix at Watkins Glen, New York. In 1971, driving a Ferrari, he won the South African G.P. with a masterful performance.

Andretti's success resulted partly from his tremendous competitive spirit, which was evident every time he climbed into a cockpit. He could go so fast for so long because he was a very aggressive man. He was not hot-tempered like A. J. Foyt, but in his own quiet way, he burned for success perhaps more than any other driver.

Mario and his twin brother Aldo were born in 1940 in the Trieste area, which was then part of Italy, near the border of Yugoslavia. His father was a prosperous landowner and the family lived comfortably. But at the end of World War II, Trieste and the surrounding area was annexed by the Communist government of Yugoslavia and the Andretti family was stripped of its land. They fled to dispersement camps in Italy where they remained from 1948 to 1955. During four of those years, they shared a room with 17 other families.

"In our make-believe games, Aldo and I always were great racing drivers," Mario recalled. "We talked a fellow who owned a repair garage into allowing us to park cars, although neither of us had ever driven one. I could barely see out the windshield, but the first time I started a car and that wheel came to life in my hands, I was hooked. I still get that same feeling every time I get into a race car."

The Andretti boys' first vehicle was an old motorcycle, which they rode on the roads near their town. Their interest in racing became an obsession when they first saw the Mille Miglia, a 1,000-mile road race. Driver Alberto Ascari was an Italian national hero, a super-hero to Mario.

Aldo and Mario finally had a chance to drive a race car at 13, a year under the minimum age. The garage owner had purchased a Formula Junior, a small, inexpensive car not much larger than a go-cart, for his son. But the son didn't want to drive, and the Andretti boys were happy to take over the car.

However, their dreams of Grand Prix glory were postponed when their parents decided to migrate to the United States. The boys' uncle lived in Nazareth, Pennsylvania, and the Andretti family settled there. Because they spoke only a little English, Mario and Aldo had difficulties in school and soon dropped out. Mario eventually earned a high school diploma through correspondence courses.

The twins soon explored the Pennsylvania racing scene and discovered the local stock car track. In 1959 they decided to convert a 1948 Hudson Hornet into a racer. They sold shares in the car to friends to get the money to complete it.

The Andrettis flipped a coin to decide who would drive the car in its first race. Aldo won and drove to a victory in the Hudson in its debut race. Mario won another race the following week. By the end of the season, they had an impressive string of victories and had won enough money to repay their backers.

In the final race of 1959 Aldo sustained serious head injuries. He recovered and continued to drive until 1969 when a crash in a sprint car race ended his career.

Mario continued to drive modified stock cars, winning 20 races during the next two years. From 1961 to 1963, he served his racing apprenticeship in sprint and midget cars. He was a big winner and his ability didn't pass unnoticed. In 1964 he was offered a chance to drive on the USAC championship trail in the Dean Van Lines Special, prepared by Clint Brawner, one of racing's best mechanics.

Andretti made his big-car debut at Trenton, New Jersey, in a 100-mile event, finishing sixth. He competed in ten championship races that season. His best finish was a third at Milwaukee. He continued to race in the sprints and placed third in the USAC sprint car series. The experts predicted that he would be U.S. racing's next big star.

In 1965 Andretti fulfilled that promise. Although he won only one race on the championship circuit, he finished second six times and earned three thirds, accumulating enough points to win the national championship. His Indianapolis 500 performance was superb as he qualified fourth and finished third behind winner Jimmy Clark and Parnelli Jones.

"At Indy that year, we didn't ventilate the cockpit properly and I almost cooked," Andretti recalled. "It was so hot in the cockpit that my biggest battle was to keep from passing out."

Although he encountered nothing but bad luck at Indianapolis during the next three years, he was U.S. racing's hot-shoe everywhere else. He won eight of 15 races in the 1966 USAC series to breeze to his second consecutive title, and was second in the sprint car series. He was fastest qualifier at Indy, but his engine went sour early in the race.

From the start, 1967 was a bad year for Andretti. In January his closest friend, driver Billy Foster, was killed in a crash during practice for a stock car race at Riverside, California. Drivers seldom become close friends, but the friendship between Andretti and Foster was an exception. Foster's death affected Andretti for a long time.

"I had to go out and qualify for the race right after Billy's crash," Andretti said. "That was the hardest thing I ever did. It was the only time when racing seemed all so meaningless. Billy and I were very close and our wives were great friends. I was shaken by it for a long, long time."

His fortunes improved during the winter series of races in Florida. He won the Daytona 500-mile stock car race against the top NASCAR drivers, then teamed with road racing star Bruce McLaren to sweep the Sebring 12-hour endurance race. But then at Indianapolis he lost a wheel on lap 58 during the race.

In June Andretti was part of the huge Ford team

in the Le Mans 24-hour race. He was running a strong fourth when a front-wheel brake locked and sent him on a wild, spinning crash. He was fortunate to escape with only a few sore ribs.

Although he won seven races on the championship trail, Andretti lost the national title to A. J. Foyt in the final race of the series at Riverside. He made a late pit stop for fuel, costing him the victory and the title. He finished 80 points behind Foyt.

To complete Andretti's luckless year of 1967, his sponsor, Al Dean of Dean Van Lines, died. Dean's will provided that the racing team be sold. Andretti bought the team, gaining financial backing from Overseas International Airways.

Operating his own team in 1968 had high and low points for Andretti. Following his third straight failure at Indianapolis, he strung together enough high finishes to battle Bobby Unser for the national championship. Again the contest went right down to the final race at Riverside. Andretti drove three different machines in the race in a frantic attempt to finish high enough to overtake Unser. However, he finished 11 points behind champion Unser in second place.

The top achievement of his career up to that point came when he accepted a ride with Team Lotus in the U.S. Grand Prix Formula 1 race at Watkins Glen, New York. From the time he had watched Alberto Ascari as a small boy in Italy, Formula 1 racing had been Andretti's big ambition.

Andretti never had driven on the tricky Watkins Glen road course, but from his first practice lap, he showed great speed. Late in the final qualifying session, he was fourth fastest, much to the surprise of the Grand Prix regulars. The big shocker was yet to come. He grabbed the pole position with a lap of 1 minute, 4.2 seconds, nearly 1½ seconds faster than Graham Hill's qualifying record.

"Everyone knew Andretti was good, and fast, too," said Grand Prix ace Jackie Stewart. "No one earns the pole in his first try at Formula 1 racing, but Andretti did it. Another thing you don't do is pick up half a second per lap that quickly, but he did that, too."

Andretti dropped out with clutch problems after 32 laps in the race. Jackie Stewart won, but Mario had made a tremendous impression on the world's auto racing elite.

Andretti qualifies for the pole position in the 1968 U.S. Grand Prix.

Andretti and Andy Granatelli joined forces in 1969 following lengthy negotiations. Granatelli's STP organization purchased Andretti's operation and gave him one of the best contracts ever acquired by a driver. The association was beneficial to both men as they won their first Indy 500. Andretti also won eight other races on the championship trail to collect the national title with a record point total and a record $287,948 in prize money.

The next two years saw Andretti achieve only a modicum of success in the Granatelli backed cars, both at Indianapolis and on the national championship trail. Still, his racing horizons were broadening considerably. He entered five Grand Prix races in 1970, driving a Granatelli-sponsored March-Ford. He finished only one event, placing third in the Spanish G.P.

Early in his career, Andretti confided to a friend that his biggest dream was to drive for Ferrari, the fabled Italian manufacturer. His childhood racing hero, Ascari, had won two world championships in Ferrari cars. In 1966 Enzo Ferrari asked Andretti to drive for him. But Mario was just getting established in USAC racing and the offer from Ferrari involved moving to Italy. Andretti turned it down. But in the 1971 season, Andretti joined the Ferrari Formula 1 team and continued his association with Granatelli in the U.S. championship series.

The Ferrari P-12 appeared to be a contender for the world championship and the Ferrari driving team was one of the strongest ever assembled—Andretti, Jackie Ickx of Belgium and Clay Regazzoni of Switzerland. The last Ferrari driver to win the world championship was John Surtees in 1963, but the driver-car combination for 1971 seemed certain to end that victory drought.

In the opening world championship race, the South African Grand Prix at the Kyalami track, Andretti qualified fourth and then won his first Formula 1. Denis Hulme in his McLaren had the lead with only three laps remaining. Then a nut worked loose in the McLaren's suspension radius rod. Andretti passed Hulme's ailing car to take the lead and go on to the victory. His lifelong dream was realized: he had won a Grand Prix race.

"Many people asked me which was the greater thrill—winning the Indianapolis 500 or a Formula 1 race," Andretti said. "I can't say one was a bigger kick than the other. Let's just say I'm a very lucky fellow to have done both. Not many people have."

Andretti realizes a long-time dream, driving a Ferrari (#2) in the Six Hour Continental at Daytona.

The remainder of 1971 was a disappointment for Andretti. The German-built McNamara cars he drove for Granatelli on the USAC circuit were extremely unreliable. At Indianapolis he completed only 11 laps when he spun on some oil and rammed another car. He finished ninth in the national driver standings, the worst ranking of his career.

In the Grand Prix series the fast Ferrari start turned sour. The cars were plagued with mechanical problems and were unable to compete with the Tyrrell cars which carried Jackie Stewart to the world title. Andretti earned points in only one other Grand Prix, taking fourth place in the race at Nurburgring, Germany.

At the end of the year he parted with Granatelli and signed with Parnelli Jones' team for the 1972 USAC series, joining Al Unser and Joe Leonard on a brilliant driving team.

Despite his mediocre 1971 season, Andretti's enthusiasm for auto racing remained at its usual high level. He lived in a beautiful home in Nazareth, Pennsylvania, with his wife and their three children. But he spent only 60 days there per year due to his heavy racing, testing and personal appearance schedule.

"If I stay home one weekend, I become irritable," Andretti said. "I can't help it but if there's a race in Timbuktu, I've got to be there. I want to keep driving for as long as I can. I figure I was put on this earth to drive race cars.

"I love race cars and that's why I get involved with so many different types of them. One of the great thrills in my life is being given a new race car that is very sophisticated and making it perform to the utmost of my capabilities. I admire versatility more than any single skill in racing. I always wanted to be an all-round driver who can handle any kind of equipment on any surface.

"It's simple, really. I enjoy racing. It's my profession, my business. My life is no bed of roses, but it's the one I've chosen. From the time I was a little boy in Italy, becoming a race driver was the only ambition I ever had. I don't really know why I race. It's just something I can't explain. I would give up everything—my home, my family, everything I've gained—to stay in racing."

5

Bruce McLaren

The 1970 Indianapolis 500 was a discouraging experience for Bruce McLaren. Long famous for his design of cars for other types of racing, he had designed and built his first Indy cars in his factory at Colnbrook, England. The machinery was very promising, but even before the race McLaren began having trouble with drivers.

First, Chris Amon quit the McLaren Indy team, claiming he couldn't make the car go fast enough. Then McLaren's top driver, Denis Hulme, suffered severe burns to his hands in a freak practice accident and was unable to drive in the race.

McLaren recruited U.S. drivers Peter Revson and Carl Williams to handle the cars in the race. The engine blew on Revson's car after 87 laps. Williams carefully motored to a ninth-place finish. For a hard-driving perfectionist like McLaren, the showing was completely unsatisfactory.

On June 2, 1970, three days after the 500, McLaren was at the Goodwood track in England to test the new McLaren M8D-Chevrolet, the car he and Hulme would drive in the Canadian-American Challenge Cup series for big sports racing cars.

They had dominated the Can-Am during the previous three seasons. McLaren was Can-Am champion in 1967 and 1969 and Hulme won the title in 1968. Between them, the two New Zealanders had won 20 of 23 races during the three-year period. One big reason for their success was McLaren's talent as a designer and builder of top racing cars.

The McLaren M8D-Chevrolet was a refinement of the previous McLaren models. With new improvements in their construction, the McLaren cars seemed sure to continue their dominance of the North American series, which offered more than $1,000,000 in prize money.

The crew had the car prepared for the test session when McLaren arrived at the track late in the morning. He had already tested the car which Hulme would drive before traveling to Indianapolis. Now he planned to give his own car the final shakedown before the team moved to Canada for the opening Can-Am race at Mosport Park in mid-June.

The Goodwood track had been built on a World War II airfield. No races had been staged there since 1966, but many racing teams used the track for tests. McLaren ran a few laps in the car, then pulled into the pits for minor adjustments. He was enthusiastic about the car's performance but wanted to correct a slight understeer.

At 12:19 p.m., after 90 minutes in the pits, McLaren drove out on the track. He gradually built up speed and roared past the pits going nearly full-speed, heading down the main straightaway towards a turn. As he approached the turn at 170 miles per

These are the skid marks of the car that took Bruce McLaren to his death during a practice run at Goodwood, England.

hour, a rear body section on the car lifted and the machine went into an uncontrollable spin. It slammed into a bank and disintegrated. At 33, Bruce McLaren died.

The death of a top driver is always a shock to the racing world. The news of McLaren's fatal crash struck especially hard in all corners of the sport. McLaren was an excellent driver who had compiled an enviable record in Formula 1 racing (four Grand Prix victories), endurance racing and the Can-Am circuit. He was also a brilliant designer and builder of racing cars. As a designer he applied a top engineering background, his skill as a test driver, and his ability to assemble and work with a highly qualified team of technicians and drivers.

Although he had failed in his first try at Indianapolis, most observers believed that he would soon succeed, adding still another championship to his successes in the Grand Prix series and the Can-Am. He was clearly one of racing's most versatile and successful young men.

McLaren's friendly, easy-going manner gave him immense popularity in a sport where enemies were much easier to obtain than friends. Other drivers found him willing to offer advice and aid in the preparation of their cars. Writers and broadcasters always received courteous treatment when they approached him for interviews.

"I don't think there's anyone on the sport who wasn't hurt by Bruce's death," said veteran U.S. driver George Follmer. "He was a superb, tough competitor but I doubt if he had an enemy in racing. I can't think of any driver who ever was more popular than Bruce."

The McLaren influence and tradition did not end with his death. His organization continued its great success in 1970 and 1971. Team McLaren dominated the Can-Am series in both years. The 1971 McLaren Indy cars were very fast, called by some experts the finest machines ever to appear at the Indianapolis Motor Speedway.

As a designer and builder, McLaren did not attempt radical new departures in his cars. Instead, he started with a solid basic design and slowly refined it with painstaking skill. His many talents made him so effective. Using his engineering background, he helped design and assemble the chassis. Then he tested the car as a top driver. His driving ability and familiarity with race conditions permitted him to detect the tiniest flaw in any car.

"I'm not a great innovator in car construction," McLaren said, during a successful Can-Am season. "But as I progressed in the building of cars, I became willing to try things that I wouldn't have attempted earlier because I had more confidence in my ability."

The strong point of the McLaren cars was their reliability. The McLaren team placed great importance on finishing the race, since even the fastest car will not win if it doesn't finish. In Can-Am competition, finishing 50 per cent of the races was a good record, but it wasn't good enough for Team McLaren. In the first 49 races in the Can-Am (1966–1971) Team McLaren cars finished more than 75 per cent of their races and won 37 times.

"There's an old racing cliché that says: before you can finish first, you first have to finish," McLaren said. "It's very true. The first move a racing team must make is to have its cars built in plenty of time for a good test program to iron out the bugs. Then,

McLaren drives one of his cars in the Can-Am series in 1969.

you must get to the races in time to set up your cars
for that particular track. They must have the reliability factor to finish the race, plus being competitive.

"It's very easy to theorize about building a revolutionary race car. I remember one time when we
were first getting started in the car construction field
and working in an old garage beside a road grader. I
heard one big builder discussing the new car he
planned. He talked in very technical terms about
the advanced techniques they planned to use in
building it. Well, I figured if he was going to build a
car that way, we might just as well forget about it in
our little operation. That fancy car never made it off
the drawing board and I learned then not to worry
about fancy ideas until I saw them on the track.

"The more deeply I became involved with automobiles, the more I realized that I knew less and less about them. Many people who are excellent with cars went through this period. I once heard someone say that it was better to be uninformed than ill-informed and I really believe that. Too many people in racing say, 'I know all about it. I can handle it.' They should be saying: 'I just don't know. I'll ask. I'll find out.' "

Perhaps the best evaluation of McLaren the builder came from Jim Hall of Texas, whose Chaparral cars often gave Team McLaren stiff competition. Hall pioneered the use of automatic transmissions in race cars and perfected the first aerodynamic wing.

"Bruce McLaren builds an unremarkable race car remarkably well," Hall said.

McLaren was born in Auckland, New Zealand, in 1937, the son of a prosperous service station and garage operator. His father, Les McLaren, was a good motorcycle racer at the local level. Later he drove sports cars in the hill climbs and beach races that were popular in New Zealand.

Young Bruce was the captain of his school's rugby football team and his major boyhood ambition was to become a member of New Zealand's famed rugby team, the "All Blacks." But when he was nine years old he contracted Perthes' Disease, an ailment of the joints, as a result of a fall from a horse. His hip joint began to shrivel and McLaren was crippled.

Young Bruce spent three years in a home for crippled children. For a while there were grave doubts that he would ever walk again. His legs in casts, he spent months flat on his back before he was allowed to use a wheelchair.

"Sure, it was very depressing, but we did manage some fun," McLaren recalled. "One night, several of us kids in wheelchairs sneaked out of the home and had a great old race over the paths of the gardens. One boy wound up in the flower bed. But we made it back inside without being detected."

When he was 11, McLaren abandoned the wheelchair and learned to walk again. The only mark left by the disease was that his left leg was more than an inch shorter than the right. He compensated with a built-up heel in his shoe, but he walked with a swinging limp all his life.

Because Bruce was unable to participate in action sports, his father allowed him to drive cars around the garage. Soon after he acquired his driver's license at 15, he and his father shared the driving in hill climbs and beach races. During the next few years, McLaren developed into one of New Zealand's best sports car drivers. He also enrolled in the engineering course at Auckland University.

The keen young McLaren became good friends with Jack Brabham, the splendid Australian driver who was to become a three-time world champion. Brabham was driving for the Cooper team in Europe. One winter he brought two Cooper formula cars to New Zealand and Australia for a series of races. Bruce drove the second car against Brabham. McLaren's talent as a driver was soon evident.

The major turning point in McLaren's career came in 1958. He became the first winner of the

Driver To Europe award of the New Zealand Grand Prix Association. The winner of this award received a trip to Europe, introductions to top racing teams, and money to cover expenses for a season of big league racing. McLaren had a year left at the university, but the chance to try racing's top competition ended his formal education.

Accompanied by a young mechanic, Colin Beanland, who later headed the engine department of Team McLaren, Bruce went to England. Jack Brabham had arranged for him to drive in a Formula 2 Cooper at the Aintree course. Although he finished in ninth place, McLaren's career in the big leagues was started.

McLaren's driving and mechanical ability was evident from the start. He sold the older Cooper he had brought from New Zealand and invested in a new model which he and Beanland assembled in a corner of the Cooper garage. He won several F.2 races and the racing world began to take notice. The New Zealander was only 20 years of age and he appeared to be even younger.

In the German Grand Prix at Nurburgring in August 1958, McLaren entered racing's front ranks. The big Formula 1 cars and smaller Formula 2 models competed together on the 14.2-mile track, one of the most difficult in the world. McLaren easily won the Formula 2 division of the race and was fifth overall behind the Formula 1 cars of Tony Brooks, Roy Salvadori, Maurice Trintignant and Wolfgang Von Tripps, the top world-class drivers. McLaren's success made him well-known in European racing circles and he was signed up to drive a

Cooper Formula 1 car for the following season.

In 1959 Jack Brabham was number one Cooper driver and McLaren and Masten Gregory were his teammates. Young Bruce drove extremely well against the world's best in the Grand Prix series and continued F.2 racing. His first major victory came in the U.S. Grand Prix at Sebring, Florida. At 22, he became the youngest driver in history to win a world championship race.

Brabham, who had won the world championship in 1958 and 1960, quit the Cooper team in 1961 to build his own cars. McLaren became the top man on the Cooper team. But the Cooper team feared that Brabham had taken many of its secrets. To keep this from happening again, they closed the design office to McLaren. In the next six years McLaren won an occasional race (Buenos Aires 1960, Monaco 1962), but he was frustrated by being shut out of the design part of the business. Cooper was not keeping up with other car builders, and McLaren seemed unable to win with the factory models.

In 1964 McLaren made his first breakthrough as a builder. He decided to construct a pair of Cooper cars for the Tasman series of winter races in New Zealand and Australia. McLaren planned to drive these cars along with a talented young U.S. driver, Tim Mayer.

But Cooper balked at the cost of the operation and refused to pay for it. McLaren and Teddy Mayer, Tim's brother, decided to share the costs themselves and enter as Bruce McLaren Motor Racing Limited. McLaren incorporated many of his own ideas into the cars, which were the first to carry his own emblem.

Jack Brabham had also built two cars for the Tasman Series and engaged New Zealander Denis Hulme as second driver. The series turned into a lively McLaren-Brabham battle. McLaren won the series but there was little joy in victory. In practice for the final race, Tim Mayer was killed when his car went off the track and slammed into a tree.

McLaren remained with the Cooper team until 1966 while he and Ted Mayer were preparing to field their own team. McLaren's main interest was big sports cars. Mayer, a law graduate from Yale University, added his business knowledge to McLaren's design and construction ability in a perfect partnership arrangement. Top mechanic Tyler Alexander joined the organization and the nucleus of Team McLaren was formed.

Bruce McLaren.

The team's first goal was the construction of a competitive sports car to compete in the big money races in North America. In 1964 they had bought the Zerex Special, which had been built and raced by Roger Penske. McLaren rebuilt it and powered it with an Oldsmobile engine and in his second race with the car, he won over Jim Clark's Lotus 30 at Aintree.

At first the rebuilt Zerex Special was called the Cooper-Oldsmobile because Bruce was still associated with the Cooper team. He won several sports car races in the car, both in North America and Europe, and moved his construction operation from the old grader shed to a new shop. Late in the 1965 season, the first 100 per cent McLaren chassis was completed and another new model was started.

When several independent North American sports car races were grouped together as the Canadian-American Challenge Cup in 1966, McLaren and his team driver Chris Amon were ready with new machines. However, their Oldsmobile engines were no match for the Chevrolet power-plants of John Surtees. McLaren finished third in the six-race series behind Surtees and Mark Donohue. That same year McLaren and Amon teamed up to win the Le Mans 24 Hours of Endurance race in Ford equipment.

Also in 1966, the McLaren Formula 1 cars made their debut, but without much success. The Ford engines in the F.1 were under-powered, so McLaren switched to Italian Serenissima engines in mid-season. He scored his first Grand Prix point in his own car with a sixth-place finish in the British G.P.

Denis Hulme, who had followed McLaren as a Driver To Europe award winner, joined Team McLaren as a driver in both the Can-Am and Formula 1 series in 1967. The Can-Am cars were powered by Chev engines and Hulme and McLaren dominated the Can-Am series. Bruce was champion in 1967 with Denis in second place, then they reversed the places in 1968, winning five of six races.

When the Can-Am expanded to 11 events in 1969, Team McLaren swept the series. Hulme won six races and collected $160,970. McLaren won five events and $151,134. More than half of the Can-Am fields consisted of McLaren cars of varying vintage.

The team's Formula 1 exploits never equaled its Can-Am achievements, although Hulme was in contention for the 1968 world championship until the final race of the series.

Carrying on the McLaren tradition, Dan Gurney drives a Team McLaren car to victory after McLaren's death.

"You must remember that many constructors have been building Formula 1 cars for a long time and you just don't catch up overnight," McLaren said. "If the same situation existed in Can-Am racing, we wouldn't be running the show. I'm enjoying it while I can because success, above all else, doesn't last forever."

McLaren's influence continued even after his death. Led by Ted Mayer, Team McLaren continued to construct cars and compete in Formula 1, Can-Am and Indianapolis racing with considerable success.

"Bruce had set high personal, moral and ethical standards for the team," said Team McLaren executive Phil Kerr. "The team didn't mind working hard because they knew Bruce worked harder than anyone."

Following the death of Tim Mayer in 1964, McLaren had written a few sentences that supplied the best possible epitaph for himself.

"The news that Tim had died instantly was a terrible shock to all of us, but who is to say that he had not seen more, done more and learned more in his few years than many people do in a lifetime? To do something well is so worthwhile that to die trying to do it better cannot be foolhardy. It would be a waste of life to do nothing with one's ability, for I feel that life is measured in achievement, not in years alone."

Don Garlits

Drag racing began nearly 50 years ago on the dry lake beds of southern California when the races were between souped-up Model T Fords. Today there are a multitude of dragster classes, 6,000 sanctioned events each year, more than one million participants, and $5 million in prize money. Drag racing attracts 10 million spectators annually and has jumped into the front ranks of North American spectator sports.

Each weekend, at drag strips ranging from the multimillion-dollar plants at Ontario, California, and Indianapolis Raceway Park, where crowds of 150,000 view top meets, down to small plants in little towns all over the country, hundreds of competitors wheel their cars through the most basic competition—a quarter-mile, straight-line race from a standing start, a simple test of pure acceleration.

The staging of a drag race is very simple. Two cars pull up to a starting line with a "Christmas tree" between them. The "tree" is actually a pole with a series of lights arranged from top to bottom. When the race is about to start, the top light, colored yellow, flashes on. Then the other lights, all yel-

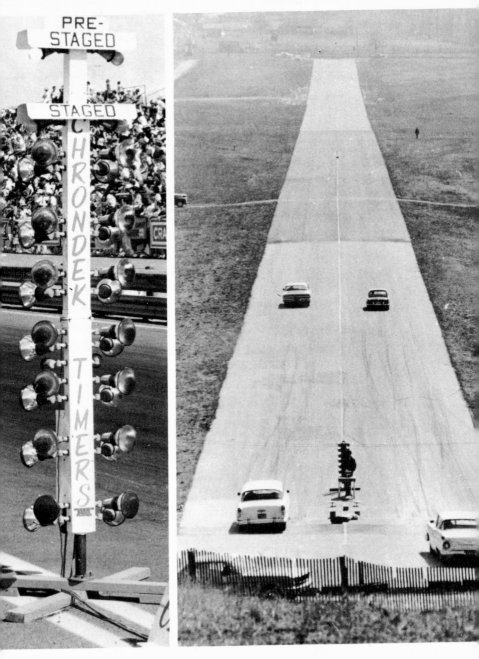

A "Christmas tree" (left) and a level stretch of pavement (right) are the necessary equipment for drag racing.

low and each one progressively brighter, flash down the pole until the green light at the bottom comes on. At that instant two cars, their back wheels spinning wildly, shoot down the 1,320-foot paved strip. Electrical timing equipment measures their top speed and elapsed time. If a car moves over the line too soon, a red light on the "tree" signals its elimination.

Although the competition is simple, the top dragsters are amazing single-purpose vehicles, designed especially to gain every last bit of speed over a quarter-mile run. Amateurs may drive their own passenger cars to the drag strip, pass a technical inspection and compete in a stock car section of the races. But drag racing's most important class is the top fuel dragster. A top fuel car is constructed from tubular steel and has a wheelbase of more than 200 inches. A supercharged engine sends more than 1,600 horsepower to extra-wide rear tires. These strange machines can travel the quarter mile in slightly more than six seconds, reaching a top speed of 240 miles per hour. At the end of the run, a parachute blossoms from the rear of the car to slow it to a safe speed.

Drag racing has its own special language. The chatter in the pit can hardly be understood by an outsider. There are abbreviations and substitutes for technical terms and a succession of nicknames for leading participants. The biggest nickname of all in the early 1970s belonged to the biggest man in drag racing. He was called "Big Daddy," and his name was Don Garlits. Through two decades, his performance on the drag strips of North America made him the undisputed king of the top fuel dragsters. He had reigned over the sport longer than any driver in any type of racing.

"Our sport has many big guns, many splendid drivers who are also excellent constructors and men who have been big winners," wrote one drag racing enthusiast. "But Garlits is 'Big Daddy.' He's unique because he's maintained his position as the best in the business for almost 20 years. There's just no other name that would fit him properly. He's 'Big Daddy,' that's all."

A quiet, intense, unpretentious man, Garlits won nine national titles through 1971, including three National Hot Rod Association (NHRA) championships. He pioneered many improvements in Class AA fueler construction. Perhaps most important was the first successful rear-engined car, which he drove to victory in the 1971 Winternationals.

Ten months earlier, Garlits had sustained serious injuries when the engine of his old front-engined dragster exploded during a run at Long Beach, California. The car ripped in half, both Garlits' legs were broken, and the toes had to be amputated from one foot. Other builders had tried the rear-engined dragster with little success. But his accident had made Garlits determined to build a safer car.

"When something went wrong in a front-engined car with the driver sitting behind the motor, everything happened in front of him—fire and danger of flying debris," he said. "I wanted to build a safer car, so I closed my mind to the failures of the others who had tried the rear-engined concept."

When he was released from the hospital, Garlits began to build the rear-engined car. By using air foils on the front and rear, he was able to stabilize

Don Garlits' top fuel dragster blows up on a run in Long Beach, California. Garlits suffered serious injuries.

the vehicle with aerodynamic downthrust which helped hold the car on the road and improve the steering. When he first appeared at a drag meet with the rear-engined car, his competitors were skeptical, although they realized that if Big Daddy had built the machine, it had to have merit. Garlits drove the car to two important victories in 1971 and the rear-engined revolution became a reality.

Garlits' contribution to drag racing's popularity extended far beyond his great driving performances and his technical innovations. As the game's top star, his name sold tickets wherever he appeared. Promoters were eager to pay him healthy fees to appear at their strips and compete against the top local drivers. Garlits enjoyed chatting with fans and other racers in the pits. Whenever he worked on his cars, a large crowd surrounded the vehicle, asking questions, seeking autographs and taking pictures. Garlits was happy to oblige because he felt an obligation to promote the sport.

"Because I've won a lot of titles and have the big name, I'm a bit like the old gunfighter in the old West," Garlits explained. "When I appear at a drag strip, people expect to see something exceptional. If I'm a bust, then they say that the advertising about 'Big Daddy' was so much baloney.

"When I'm at a strip, many other drivers come around to see what I'm doing with my car, what changes I've made to make it go faster. The real race fans can spot any tiny changes in the car and they pull me and the car apart to find out what I'm doing. I like that. To the other drivers, I'm the hired professional gun. They all want to knock me off, but

Don "Big Daddy" Garlits.

that's what keeps me working to improve. Being at the top means everyone is gunning for you and it pushes you to be just a little better than anyone else."

Because of the incredible speeds and the enormous power of the huge engines, drag racing is a dangerous sport. The cars and drivers are subjected to tremendous stress. When a car travels at 230 miles per hour, the slightest mechanical failure or driver error could send it into a disintegrating crash.

"For me, success and survival come from refining the car and power-plant to the stage where I get away just a bit quicker, move a bit faster, stay together and stop," Garlits said. "The difference between the top cars is measured in the smallest possible fractions.

"When I'm driving, I can't give away the little edges I've gained when building the cars. The stress on my cars is unbelievable and they're like bullets. I'm traveling at 300 feet per second so if anything goes wrong, it happens very quickly. At those speeds, I can't make a mistake, such as hitting the brakes too soon or not pulling the chute release at the proper instant."

Garlits was born in Tampa, Florida. As a teenager he was interested only in automobiles. When he graduated from high school, he worked in an office for six months, then quit to become involved with cars. He worked as a mechanic until he saved enough money to open his own small garage. Garlits made his drag racing debut in a modified stocker, then branched into the construction of his own pure drag racing machinery.

Garlits quickly rose to the top of the local Florida drag ranks and in 1955 he scored his first major victory at the NHRA "Safety Safari." In an attempt to promote interest in drag racing and organize a strong national governing body, the NHRA had assembled a group of drivers to tour the country, staging meets against local racers and instructing strip officials in the proper way to conduct the sport. Driving his top fuel "Swamp Rat," Garlits scored a surprise win over Joe Travis, one of the sport's big names.

From that start, Garlits quickly moved towards his "Big Daddy" status. His early cars were roughly constructed, lacking the beauty of the chrome-plated, technically proper machines run by bigger drivers.

"When I first raced in California, they called me

'Don Garbage' because my cars were less than gorgeous compared to the slick California machines," Garlits recalled. "They used to laugh at me, but not for long, because I cleaned up on a lot of those fancy-looking machines."

Garlits never concerned himself with building fancy-looking cars. His pure, straightforward machines stressed strength rather than beauty, durability instead of chrome. He quickly became a man who established the sport's standards. He was the first racer to crash the 170 mph top speed barrier. The 200 mph mark then became the major target, and Garlits broke it, too.

Topping the 170 mark was a major turning point in Garlits' career. When word of his achievement spread through the sport, promoters wanted him to appear at their strips.

"That's when I became a professional," he said. "If they wanted me to appear, they had to pay me a fee. In those days, there wasn't much competition, only a few top cars. I'd go to a track and compete with the top local boys. The promoter would be happy because he sold a lot of tickets and the spectators were pleased because they'd watched me beat the strip record and shut down the local hot-shots. It was the old hired gunslinger idea, but it helped me get established in the sport.

"But, as drag racing gained popularity, the competition gradually became very stiff. Before long, there were plenty of good cars and excellent drivers, and a lot of different winners in the big races. It became a question of working hard to gain a little edge here and there in building the cars and the same in driving them. I believe that any success I've had was because I always worked on my own cars, from the design boards to the strip. I knew them inside out, how much stress they could take and the way to correct any small problems."

In the late 1950s Garlits began to win the big meets, starting with the NHRA Safety Safari in 1958 and the American Hot Rod Association (AHRA) Summernationals the same year. In 1963 he won the NHRA Winternationals and the NHRA top fuel eliminator title a year later. He took the NHRA National title again in 1967 and 1968 to become a three-time winner and the first to win two years in a row.

Garlits never allowed his construction program to stagnate. He continually tried to incorporate new ideas into the cars to maintain that step ahead of his competitors. In 1970, when he was 38 years old and had 16 years of top-level competition behind him, he appeared to have the car to retain his position.

He scored a decisive victory in the AHRA Winternationals and in March 1970, he appeared to be on his way to a win in the AHRA Grand American Championship in California. Then came his near-tragic run in Long Beach. The engine disintegrated, splitting the car in half. Garlits' serious injuries caused much speculation that his career, at least as a driver, might be over. But three months later "Big Daddy" was on the line at the AHRA Spring-national meet. Then in February 1971, less than a year after the crash, he scored an easy victory in the Winternational meet at Pomona, California, in his revolutionary rear-engined car.

"This is the first rear-engined car with all the right ingredients," Garlits said. "No one who tried the design before me had the new clutches and tires that were available to me, and my car is longer [215 inches] than the early rear-engined models, and

Two views of Garlits' revolutionary rear-engined dragster.

lighter by about 250 pounds [total weight: 1,250 pounds].

"Also, having the engine behind me allowed me to use rear-view mirrors to good advantage. They're set up so I can view the engine and the exhaust. If the exhaust doesn't look right, I shut down because there's no point in losing an engine. In this car I get a clear view of what's ahead, a big change from the old car where on almost every run I had water, oil, fuel spray and fumes all over me and I never had a good view. I'll never drive a front-engined machine again."

There appeared to be no end in sight to the fabulous Garlits drag racing career. He often was asked why he didn't try other forms of auto racing on ovals or road courses.

"Well, I never was particularly interested in driving any other type of cars, say at Indianapolis," he replied. "Drag racing has been my field, the area that I know about, so I stuck with it. It's too late now to think of changing. I've been the big man in drag racing and I've enjoyed that. I make a good living out of the sport and have a little money tucked away. My Hi Performance World speed shop in Tampa is successful.

"I have a good wife, a fine family and a nice home in Florida, although I don't spend much time there because I travel about 150,000 miles a year. Sometimes my family and I live like gypsies, travelling around to drag meets, but we enjoy it. I'm a big man to the fans; the other drivers respect me. That's important to me. I'm in the sport. I enjoy it. It's my life."

7

Mark Donohue

Mark Donohue's ascent to the top of the auto racing world was not merely the story of one man's climb up the ladder of success. It was the tale of two men whose careers in auto racing were intertwined so closely as to be inseparable.

One of the men was Donohue, a boyish-looking, quiet college graduate in engineering. His engineering background allowed him to participate in every phase of racing—design, construction, testing and racing. And his amazing versatility as a race driver permitted him to win in nearly every form of racing —big sports cars of the Can-Am series, Trans-Am sedans, endurance events, Formula A cars on road courses and the big Indianapolis cars on the U.S. Auto Club championship trail. Donohue's nickname was "Captain Nice."

The second man was intense, ambitious Roger Penske, a winning race driver who retired unexpectedly in the early 1960s. A very successful businessman in a variety of areas, Penske formed Penske Racing Enterprises, the most efficient team in racing, and Donohue was his number one driver. Penske's nickname was "Captain"—as in "Captain

Bligh," said his crew members with a smile.

Donohue and Penske joined forces in 1966 and compiled an enviable record of racing achievements. Most remarkable was that they finished more than 80 per cent of the races they started.

Driving cars under the Penske banner, Donohue won the U.S. Road Racing Championship series for big sports cars in 1967 and 1968. In the Can-Am series the Penske organization compiled the best record of any American team. As a driver, Donohue placed second to Can-Am champion John Surtees in 1966 and third behind the powerhouse Team McLaren drivers, Bruce McLaren and Denis Hulme, in 1967 and 1968.

The Trans-American Sedan championship was almost the personal property of Donohue and the Penske team. Driving Chevrolet Camaros, Donohue won the title in 1968 (10 wins in 13 races) and 1969 (6 wins in 12 events). Switching to American Motors' Javelins in 1970, he was second to Ford in the Trans-Am. However, he won the 1971 series for Javelin with victories in 7 of 10 races.

In 1969 Donohue teamed with Chuck Parsons to win the Daytona 24-hour endurance race in the Penske-Lola. The Penske team also made its Indianapolis 500 debut that year. Donohue qualified in the second row and finished seventh to win rookie of the year honors. In 1970 he finished second to Al Unser at Indy.

Then in 1971, driving a McLaren on a practice run, Donohue ran the fastest lap ever recorded at the Indianapolis Motor Speedway—a fraction under 181 miles per hour, almost 10 miles per hour faster

Mark Donohue sets a new lap record at Indianapolis in 1971.

than the record qualifying speed. Eventually, he qualified second for the race and was leading by more than a mile when forced out of the race by a broken gearbox after 66 laps.

Later in 1971 Donohue acquired his first major USAC championship win with an easy victory in the 500-mile race on the new track at Pocono, Pennsylvania, and added a win in a 200-miler at Michigan International Speedway. And in September he made his Formula 1 debut, driving a McLaren-Ford in the Canadian Grand Prix at Mosport Park, finishing third in the rain behind world champion Jackie Stewart and Ronnie Peterson.

The Donohue-Penske partnership was ideal because their talents and temperaments blended perfectly. Penske controlled the business side of the operation. He arranged sponsorship, purchased the cars, hired the super-efficient staff for the team and supervised the entire operation. With those facets of the team well looked after, Donohue could concentrate on preparing and racing the cars. Both men had a passion for detail, a burning ambition to succeed and great competitive desire. Penske was outspoken and emotional, while Donohue preferred to keep his thoughts and opinions to himself.

"The way they work together is a strange thing," said one Penske team crew member. "Although they are very different people, they have a sort of mental telepathy between them that allows them to agree on the correct decision very quickly. They both are very meticulous in paying attention to every detail, no matter how small."

Penske graduated from Lehigh University in 1959 with a degree in industrial management. While employed as a sales engineer for an aluminum company, he became one of the best U.S. road racers. As an amateur he twice won Sports Car Club of America (SCCA) national championships.

Penske won the 1962 Times Grand Prix sports car race at Riverside, California, the richest American road race at the time. U.S. racing fans predicted he would become the world champion. However, at the end of the 1964 season, after he won all three races during Nassau Speed Week, Penske retired from racing at the age of 26.

"I quit because there was greater opportunity for me in business," Penske said. "To remain in racing, I had to make too many commitments to banks and investment people."

Penske quickly established a business empire which he claimed was the result of his racing endeavors. He operated three automobile dealerships and an import car franchise, a Goodyear racing tire distributorship and a car and truck rental company. He owned an office building and was a consultant

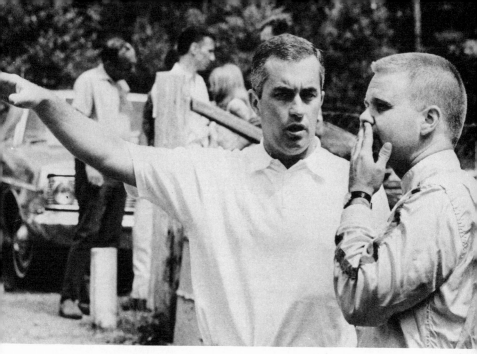

Roger Penske (left) and Donohue talk over an upcoming race.

for Sears, Roebuck and Company, which features special Penske performance products for autos. It was estimated the Penske business operations grossed $50,000,000 in 1971.

"My approach to business is the same as it is to auto racing," Penske explained. "I pay attention to detail and surround myself with good people."

Born in Summit, New Jersey, in 1937, Donohue graduated in mechanical engineering from Brown University in 1959. He started racing that year, driving a Corvette to a hill climb victory in his first try at the sport. His considerable driving talent showed from the start. He seemed to know how to win a race without running his car beyond its abilities. A consistent winner in amateur sports car racing, he won an SCCA national title in 1961, driving an Elva-Courier.

Donohue won the SCCA Driver of the Year award in 1965 for his two national championships in a Mustang and a Lotus. He was ready for racing's big leagues. A year later, he teamed with Walt Hansgen, one of the best U.S. sports car drivers, and they drove a Mark II Ford to third place in the Daytona 24-hour race and second place in the Sebring 12-hour event. Hansgen was killed in a crash during practice for the 1966 Le Mans 24-hour race.

By this time, Penske had his Sunoco-sponsored racing team well organized and was seeking a driver to handle his Lola-Chevrolet in the 1966 Canadian-American Challenge Cup series. He hired Donohue and racing's perfect partnership was formed. The car made its debut in the U.S. Road Racing Championship (USRRC) event at Kent, Washington, and Donohue won handily.

The Can-Am featured a strong field of international drivers in 1966, its first year of existence. The series consisted of six races over a two-month period. John Surtees and Dan Gurney had Lolas, Jim Hall and Phil Hill drove Chaparrals while Bruce McLaren and Chris Amon handled the Team McLaren cars.

The first Penske-Donohue series in the big leagues already showed their strengths. The Penske crew had the Lola prepared immaculately and Donohue supplied his steady driving to finish and acquire points in five of the six races. Surtees won three races to become the first Can-Am champ with 27 points. In the race at Mosport Park Donohue won in a battle of attrition. The front-runners dropped out one by one until he was in the lead. He ended the series in second place with 21 points and won $25,850.

From the start, it was obvious that Penske and Donohue were no ordinary combination. Penske always insisted that Donohue was the most underrated driver in the sport.

"Mark is the most consistent driver in the business," Penske said. "He never drives at 102 per cent, over his head, but at 98 per cent. He always has something in reserve. Our relationship was perfect for a lot of reasons. We're the same age, and he's like my brother. Mark is a dedicated, honest person who never tries to put himself out in front.

"Mark was a tremendous asset from the beginning. One of the reasons he's so good is that he can evaluate what we're doing on the drawing board, then see if it works exactly as it should be on the track. You might call him a built-in stability factor. He simply never abuses a vehicle."

The team launched a two-pronged attack in U.S. racing in 1967. They entered a new Lola-Chev in the USRRC and Can-Am series and a Chevrolet Camaro in the Trans-American Sedan championship. The USRRC series of eight races was Donohue's private domain. He won six events to finish with 54 points, leading second-place Lothar Motschenbacher by 33 points.

Donohue's Can-Am performance was below the team's par. He completed only three of the six races, but still earned two second-place finishes and one third to tie Surtees for third place in the point standings.

In the Trans-Am series, which is a manufacturer's rather than a driver's championship, Donohue had three wins, two seconds and a third, but Chevrolet finished third behind Ford and Mercury.

When the 1968 racing season rolled around, the team had assembled a superb crew of designers, builders and mechanics, guided by Penske and Donohue. Switching from a Lola to a McLaren-Chev, Donohue repeated as USRRC champion with five victories in eight races. He also supplied Chevrolet with the Trans-Am crown, winning an amazing total of 10 races in 13 tries. In the two series, Donohue finished 15 times in 21 events. And he won every race he finished!

That superb finishing percentage was continued by Donohue in the 1968 Can-Am series as he completed five of six races, winning the Bridgehampton, New York, event. Denis Hulme won the series and McLaren was second, only one point ahead of Donohue.

His 1968 mastery of the U.S. road racing scene earned Donohue the Martini and Rossi Driver of the Year award, and the Pennsylvania Junior Chamber of Commerce named him "Outstanding Young Man of 1968."

In 1969 when the USRRC ended its racing series, the Can-Am series expanded to 11 races. Penske and Donohue decided to drop out of big sports car competition.

"When the 1968 Can-Am ended, we realized that there was no competitive Can-Am car available for us to purchase that would be potentially better than anyone else in the series," Donohue said. "So Roger and I decided to evaluate some other types of racing."

Donohue (#6) takes the lead in a 1969 Trans-Am race.

The team continued to campaign the Camaros in the Trans-Am sedan series. Donohue won six races and finished second twice in 12 events, winning the title again. Parsons and Donohue drove the team Lola to victory in the Daytona 24-hour event, a rather unusual triumph because they spent almost three hours in the pits but still managed to win when the top factory entries were sidelined by mechanical problems.

The team's major 1969 effort was its first try at the Indianapolis 500 with a Lola chassis powered by a turbo-charged Offenhauser engine. Donohue was fourth fastest qualifier at 168.903 miles per hour and earned the respect of the Indy veterans with his smooth handling of the tricky Indianapolis oval.

Because of nagging mechanical problems, Donohue finished only second. But his performance showed unusual tenacity and ability to adjust to any situation. The fuel mixture Donohue used was too rich, so the engine flooded and cut out every time he stepped on the accelerator after applying the brakes. Despite this difficulty, he was running in third position on lap 172. Then a faulty magneto forced him to make a 10½-minute pit stop to have it replaced. He finished ten laps behind winner Mario Andretti but his performances in the qualifying rounds earned Donohue the Rookie of the Year award.

"I guess you shouldn't complain about a top ten finish, but you always drive to win, not just to finish high," Donohue said after the race. "The car was good but I didn't have the proper throttle response coming out of the turns because of the fuel mixture. It was quite an experience and there's no doubt that oval racing is a different game from the road courses. Oval experience is a very valuable thing here."

Penske and Donohue accepted a major challenge in 1970 when they signed a three-year contract with American Motors to field the factory team of Javelins in the Trans-Am sedan series. The opposition was formidable, headed by the Ford Mustang team of Parnelli Jones and George Follmer. The series had five victory-backed teams and a top list of drivers.

Problems in the oil-pickup apparatus, which resulted in engine failures, caused the Penske team to get away to a slow start in the first four races and allowed Ford to build a big early lead. But once the engine problems were solved, Donohue won three of four races in the middle of the series to challenge the

Fords. Jones won the final race, however, and the Ford Mustang won the title.

Several Trans-Am races featured brutal competition between Jones and Donohue, including some fender-bashing. Some fans were surprised at Donohue's aggressiveness against Jones, one of racing's most aggressive drivers.

"People seem to think that Donohue is some kind of angel on the race track," Jones commented. "Well, don't believe it. Nobody pushes him around. He can mix it up with the best of us."

Donohue blamed himself for not winning the 1970 Indianapolis 500 in his Lola, powered by a turbo-charged Ford engine. He merely finished second, 32 seconds behind winner Al Unser, after qualifying fifth fastest in another impeccable driving job.

"I set the car up for a bit of understeer which meant it would be pushing outward, away from the left-hand turns," he said. "It was a mistake and I didn't recognize that it would become an increasing problem as the race progressed. When the tires were cool, everything was fine. When they got hot and the track became slippery, it became difficult to get through the corners."

In 1971 the Trans-Am series returned to normal for the Penske team. Donohue won the manufacturer's title for Javelin with seven victories in the series. The Penske team also made another try at Indy, entering a McLaren chassis with an Offenhauser engine. Donohue tore the track speed records to shreds. The record of 171.559 miles per hour had been set in 1969 by Joe Leonard, driving a turbine-powered car. Early in practice, Donohue did laps at

177, and later was clocked at more than 180 mph. In official qualifying for the race, Donohue was second at 177 mph, nosed out for the pole position by Peter Revson in another McLaren.

But Donohue hit more bad luck. A failure in the gearbox forced him out of the race after 66 laps. He had led the pack for 52 of his 66 laps. When he quit, he parked his car on the infield near turn four. Later, two cars spun off the track and into Donohue's empty car, wrecking it completely.

With a new car, the Penske team competed in several USAC championship trail events, winning at Pocono and Michigan. In the 500-mile race at Ontario, Donohue earned the pole position with a speed of 185 mph and was leading the race when he ran out of fuel and had to push the car back to the pits. He had failed to see the pitboard sign telling him to stop.

Despite his great success in racing, Donohue changed very little through his years in tough competition. He never viewed his accomplishments as an individual achievement.

"Any success I've had has been the result of a team effort," he said. "I'm just one member of that team. Because of my engineering background, I get credit for more than I should. I work with two very talented men, Don Cox and Chuck Cantwell, in the racing operation and we all contribute ideas on the way things should be done. I do the testing, but what I discover on the test track must be translated into improvement on the car and the entire team participates."

Donohue gets a garland after winning the 1971 Pocono 500.

8

Jimmy Clark

The history of Grand Prix racing can be divided into "eras" of great drivers. These drivers made their mark on a particular period with their great driving performances and they provided the standard against which all other drivers were measured.

The early 1950s was the era of Alberto Ascari of Italy, world champion in 1952 and 1953 and winner of 13 races in three seasons as a Ferrari driver. Next came Juan Manuel Fangio, the brilliant star from Argentina, who won a record five world crowns. Fangio won four consecutive titles from 1954 to 1957. During his career, he drove Alfa-Romeo, Maserati, Mercedes-Benz and Lancia-Ferrari cars to 24 victories.

Although England's Stirling Moss never won the world championship, he was an exceptional driver of great ability, equally at home in Formula 1 or big sports cars. Fast and smooth, Moss won 16 Grands Prix between 1955 and May 1962, when injuries from a crash ended his career.

The year after Moss' retirement, Jimmy Clark, a quiet little driver from Scotland's farm country, won his first world championship. From his first Formula

1 victory in the 1962 Belgian Grand Prix until he died in a crash in 1968, Clark won 25 world championship races, passing Fangio's record of 24.

Comparing great drivers from different eras is difficult because cars and racing conditions change so quickly. But many experts rated Clark as the greatest driver in auto racing history. Clark was a smooth driver, fast and safe, who could drive just below the limits of his car's and his own capabilities.

"To compare Jimmy with the great drivers of other times is not easy, but it's true to say, I think, that in their times Fangio, Moss and Clark were the greatest," said Graham Hill, Clark's teammate for several years and twice world champion.

"Fangio was just a little quicker than Moss in a Formula 1 car, and Moss was a better all-round driver than Fangio. But Jimmy Clark won more Grand Prix races than either of them."

During his Grand Prix career Clark drove only Lotus cars, which were designed and built by Colin Chapman. Even when he won the Indianapolis 500 in 1965, the victory was in a Lotus. Clark and Chapman formed an almost perfect partnership. Although Clark had no engineering background, he was able to tell Chapman exactly the way the car was handling during test sessions. Chapman understood perfectly and translated Clark's descriptions into mechanical improvements.

"The key to Jimmy's driving success was that he was relaxed, always in charge of the situation, and he seldom drove beyond nine-tenths of his capacity," Chapman said. "He always appeared to be smooth and competent. His great natural ability permitted him to drive within himself much more than other drivers."

Several of Clark's driving performances rank among the greatest in history. In the 1962 German Grand Prix at Nurburgring, he neglected to switch on his fuel pumps and was left on the starting grid when the green flag fell. He made up much of the distance which he had lost and finished fourth.

Clark's performance in the 1967 Italian Grand Prix at Monza produced perhaps the finest driving display in the long years of the world championship series. When one of his tires was punctured, he lost a lap and a half on the race leaders while he limped back to the pits and the tire was replaced. But he came back and not only caught the leaders, but lapped the entire field.

Scotland's Jimmy Clark.

"I think it was a virtuoso drive which no other driver has ever equaled or will ever be able to surpass," Chapman said.

At Indianapolis in 1966, a year after he won the 500, he drove a car that was handling badly and twice went into spins on turn four. Both times his lightning-fast maneuvering permitted him to avoid hitting the wall. A year later in the 500, the suspension broke on his car as he headed into a turn, but he guided the damaged car to a safe stop on the infield grass, making a desperate maneuver look ridiculously easy.

Although Clark was relaxed when driving a Grand Prix car at high speed, he was high-strung and nervous out of the car and continually chewed his fingernails. He came from farm country and he never got used to the crowds of fans, autograph seekers and questioning reporters.

"The farm is the place where I can unwind," Clark once said. "The cattle don't ask for autographs and the sheep don't bother me for interviews.

"I enjoy driving a race car, but not all that other stuff," Clark said. "For the driver, every race is a new adventure. I don't just like going fast—a straight line means nothing—but there is a thrill in being in control."

Clark was a small man (5-foot-8, 160 pounds) but he was built like a good welterweight boxer, with wide shoulders and surprising strength.

"Jimmy was the best driver because he had all the requirements," Graham Hill said. "He was a natural athlete with excellent coordination and very good eyes. He was light on his feet, his judgment was excellent and his reactions were very fast. Add to this his being a splendid competitor who was very aggressive. He also had a very good sense of what not to do. Some people are so aggressive they are dangerous, but Jimmy never was this way. He was a fighter who never gave up. His favorite race strategy was to shoot into the lead and kill off the others, building such a margin that he discouraged their will to win."

Despite his remarkable ability and love for racing, like most drivers Clark went through periods when he seriously considered giving up the sport. In the 1961 Italian Grand Prix at Monza young German driver Wolfgang Von Trips was in contention for the world championship. Early in the race, Von Trips, driving a Ferrari, passed Clark. The young Scot got in behind the Ferrari to receive a "tow" in its slipstream.

When Clark broke the slip-stream and moved out to pass, Von Trips drove into his path and the cars collided. Clark's Lotus spun safely to a stop but Von Trips' Ferrari hurtled over an embankment at 150 miles per hour. Von Trips and 13 spectators were killed.

"When a thing like that happens, even though it wasn't directly your fault, you vow that you never will race again," Clark said. "But then your mind begins to function and everyday things begin to crowd their way back. Three days later, you are packing your bags for another race."

Clark never viewed his racing career as being especially glamorous. "I think racing is more of a science than a sport," he said. "People are forever ask-

ing me what it feels like. They want to know if it's
thrilling or if it's exciting. Well, I'm too busy to feel
anything. If I'm thinking anything, it's maybe that
the engine should be turning out a little more power

Clark prepares for the 1962 U.S. Grand Prix.

on a particular part of the circuit. The fact that I'm traveling 160 or 170 miles per hour means absolutely nothing to me."

Clark was born in the farming country of Scotland near Edinburgh, where his father operated three large farms. When Jim finished school he managed one of the farms, Edgington Mains, near the small town of Duns. He first became interested in car competition when he participated in rallies and sprint races at the club level. He soon was well known in the area for his wild driving on the winding, narrow country roads in an old Sunbeam Talbot.

Clark's first exposure to racing came in 1956 when he accompanied the well-known Scottish team the Border Reivers to the races, changing tires and helping in the pits. One day he drove the small DKW sedan of a regular team driver around the circuit and bettered the regular's time by three seconds per lap. Before long he was a team member himself and a superb career was underway.

Clark's family was opposed to his racing and because of this, he went through two years of indecision about making the sport his career. However, his abundant success in a variety of cars began to attract the attention of the top racing teams and it finally became clear that he would abandon the farm for the track.

In 1960 he signed with the Aston Martin team for the Formula 1 Grand Prix series and drove Formula 2 and 3 cars for Lotus. The deal with Aston Martin never came through and in June 1960, Clark made his Formula 1 debut driving a spare Team Lotus car in the Dutch Grand Prix. Clark worked his way through the field to fifth place. But the transmission locked, forcing him out of the race.

The partnership of Clark and Colin Chapman had opened on a sour note. But this alliance would dominate the world championship series for the next eight years. Chapman was a former driver who had recently retired from the track to give all his time to the design and construction of the Lotus cars.

"We came of age together," Chapman said. "Lotus had just entered Grand Prix racing and so had Jimmy. I needed a good driver, a man with whom my team could grow, and he was ideal."

Clark required only a two-year apprenticeship to move to the top of racing's toughest league. In June 1962, he won the Belgian Grand Prix, the first of his 25 world championship victories. He added wins in the British and U.S. races to enter the final event of the series in South Africa as a contender for the title. He had a good lead on Graham Hill when the Lotus developed an oil leak. Clark dropped out and Hill went on to win the race and championship.

In 1963, the Clark-Chapman duo turned the Indianapolis 500 upside down—almost. Although Indy always had been the domain of the huge front-engined roadsters, some Formula 1 people thought that the slick, rear-engined Grand Prix cars could win at Indy. Jack Brabham had entered in 1961 in an under-powered rear-engined car and performed impressively. Chapman and Clark took their little Grand Prix car to Indianapolis for secret tests in late 1962 and discovered that it was very fast.

Backed by the Ford Motor Company, Chapman
built his first Indianapolis chassis, a low, independ-

In the 1963 Indy 500, Clark (#9) takes the inside track against a bulky front-engined roadster.

ently suspended car which seemed very small next to the Indy roadsters. Clark encountered considerable hostility at Indianapolis. As a first-year driver he had to pass the "rookie test," in which his perform- ance was inspected at various speeds. His Grand Prix experience counted for nothing at Indy and Clark admitted that he found the test insulting. He qualified on the third row of the starting grid.

The race itself caused considerable argument. Clark had planned a fast start but he was caught be- hind a slow car and at the end of the first lap he was in 12th place. Because his car needed fewer pit stops than the roadsters, Clark was able to take over the lead as the race progressed.

However, Clark's strict observance of the rules cost him the race. When the yellow caution light was on, drivers were supposed to slow down and hold their position. Parnelli Jones, who was ahead of Clark, slowed down less and increased his lead. He also made his pit stops when the caution light was on. That way he lost less distance than Clark, who stopped when the light was green and the racers were going at full speed.

Near the end of the race, Clark was four seconds behind Jones, when Jones' engine began to leak oil. It was argued after the race that Jones should have been flagged off the track, since an oil leak causes a serious hazard for other drivers. But the owner of Jones' car convinced the starter to let him continue. Jones won the race but Clark had earned tremen- dous respect for his driving skill—and for his rear- engined car.

Later in the year Clark drove the Lotus Indy-car

in a 200-mile race at Milwaukee, Wisconsin, and scored an easy victory. He lapped every roadster driver in the field except A. J. Foyt. After that race, even the biggest supporters of the traditional Indy roadster were convinced that rear-engined cars would take over the series.

The Lotus-Clark superiority in Grand Prix racing was established beyond doubt as the 1963 season progressed. Clark won seven races, in a one-season record that never has been equaled, and swept the world driving championship.

However, Clark discovered in 1964 that auto racing success was difficult to keep up. He was the fastest qualifier at Indianapolis in a field dotted with rear-engined cars. But his car never performed properly in the race and he dropped out early when a tire blew out, causing the suspension to collapse. In the Grand Prix program he was hampered by a variety of nagging mechanical problems and won only three races. He finished well down the list in the final standings behind world champion John Surtees.

The highlight of the year for Clark was his becoming a member of the Order of the British Empire, an honor granted to Britons who excel in a variety of fields. Clark's parents accompanied him to Buckingham Palace for the investiture, and it was a day of tremendous pride for them all.

The 1965 season saw Clark return to his position at the top. At Indianapolis, he led the 500 for 190 of 200 laps and at the finish his margin of victory was more than three miles, one of the largest leads in the history of the race. Clark was the first non-American driver to win the 500 since 1916 and Lotus was the first rear-engined V-8 car ever to win. The Grand Prix series was again his personal hunting ground. He won six races and obtained his second world driving championship.

During the next two seasons, Clark was unable to repeat as winner at Indianapolis or as world champion. Still, he continued to win many races and was the acknowledged master of his craft. The "formula" for cars in the Grand Prix series changed in 1966, allowing engine displacement to increase from 1.5 liters to 3 liters. The Lotus team didn't have a strong engine of the larger size, and Clark was hampered by running a less competitive car.

Clark opened the 1968 season by winning the South African Grand Prix. His victory served notice that Lotus had returned to prominence with its new Ford engine. The win was the 25th of Clark's Formula 1 career which made him the greatest winner of world championship races, one victory ahead of the mighty Fangio.

Clark spent the winter in Australia and New Zealand and won the Tasman Championship series. When he returned to Europe, he appeared to be on the verge of a great season in Formula 1 and at Indianapolis where he was to drive the impressive STP-Lotus turbine car.

Clark flew his own plane to Hockenheim, West Germany, for a Formula 2 race of little importance, scheduled for April 7. He accepted the driving assignment because he wanted to help the Lotus team win the series championship. Rain fell on race day, and in the first heat Clark was running in eighth place with an engine that was producing below top power. On the fifth lap, he headed into a long, gentle curve at 150 miles per hour and the car went out of control, skidded off the track and smashed broadside into a tree. Clark died instantly.

Because of the severe damage to the car, the reason for the crash never was determined. Most people at the race agreed that the cause was mechanical failure, not driver error.

"Of one thing I'm sure—it wasn't Jim's fault at Hockenheim," said Graham Hill, who was in the same race in a second Lotus. "He simply did not make mistakes."

A policeman guards the wreckage of Clark's car after his fatal crash in 1968.

9

Parnelli Jones

In comparison to other great drivers, Parnelli Jones did not have a big list of racing victories. But he won big and he lost big, causing controversy wherever he went. In 1963 he won the Indy 500 after traveling the last laps with an oil leak. His critics said he should have been flagged off the track. Then in 1967, driving a controversial turbine car, he was ten laps from victory when the car broke down.

Those two races were typical of Parnelli's stormy racing career. He was a hard-living, hard-charging driver, one of the fiercest competitors in the sport's history. Parnelli had charisma, the ability to attract attention everywhere he went. And he had great talent in the cockpit of a racing car. These two qualities made him a super-hero in the annals of U.S. racing.

Jones arrived at the top the hard way, fighting his way through California jalopy and stock car racing, then through the U.S. Auto Club sprint car circuit and finally to the national championship trail. He was shrewd and hard-boiled, a driver who gave no inches on the track, and he was at his best in close wheel-to-wheel racing which required nerves of steel.

Parnelli Jones (left) discusses a race with his team manager.

Jones' racing career made him a wealthy man as he wisely invested his prize money. As he reduced his racing schedule in the late 1960s, he and his lifelong friend Vel Miletich fielded the cars which Al Unser drove to victory at Indianapolis in 1970 and 1971 and which carried Joe Leonard to the national driving title in 1971. Jones and Miletich also owned a Firestone tire store in California, an auto dealership, and the distributorship for racing tires in 11 states.

Although Jones had made the switch from driver to businessman, he still felt the urge to compete. In 1970, four years after his last try at Indianapolis, he displayed the incredible Jones spirit in the Trans-American Sedan series. He led the Ford Mustang team to the championship in a lively, fender-bashing series. Parnelli was in the middle of the action—and winning most of it.

"I really got a big kick out of every race I ever ran, even the losses," Jones said in 1970. "If you lose a few big ones, especially when they're snatched away from you late in the race, then you really appreciate the wins. I had a great deal of respect for the guys I raced against but I always figured that if all things were equal, I could take any of them. You have to think that way if you want to do anything in racing."

The Indianapolis Motor Speedway was the place where Jones' reputation was established. He made his driving debut there in 1961, finishing 12th. He earned the pole position a year later but finished seventh in the race.

The 1963 race was important in Indy's history because it marked the beginning of the rear-engined revolution at the Speedway. Five cars in the field of 33 were the small, rear-engined machines based on the Formula 1 cars. The remainder of the field consisted of traditional roadsters. Jones' roadster, powered by an Offenhauser engine, was owned by the famed J. C. Agajanian, and Parnelli had placed in on the pole, qualifying at a record speed of 151.3 miles per hour.

Leading the charge of the rear-engined cars was Jimmy Clark of Scotland, often considered the finest driver in the history of Grand Prix racing. The race was a clear-cut battle between the Indy establishment, who wanted the roadsters to remain the dominant Indy car, and the invaders from road racing, who sought to take control with their sophisticated rear-engined cars.

Jones knew he had to run hard because he required two pit stops for fuel and tire changes. The lighter rear-engined machines were easier on tires and used less fuel and could run the 500 miles with only one pit stop.

Parnelli demonstrated his intention of being a tough man to beat by charging into an early lead, holding it until his first pit stop on lap 64. Clark moved in front, but fell back to second during his pit stop.

Jones maintained his lead through a fast pit stop, which he made under a yellow caution flag when the field was moving at a reduced speed. With 125 miles remaining in the race, Parnelli had a 48-second margin on Clark when black smoke began to billow from the back of his car. The outside oil tank on his engine had developed a crack which allowed the lubricant to spurt out onto the hot exhaust pipes, causing the smoke. The oil also was coating one tire, making the car twitchy through the turns.

"My heart sank when the car started to wiggle in the back end," Jones recalled. "I looked back and saw that the tire was covered with oil. I thought the oil line had broken. I figured the race was gone from my grasp again. Then I slowed down and nursed the car along, trying to go as far as I could."

The track became slippery because of the oil from Jones' car, but Clark cut into Parnelli's lead on every lap until he was only four seconds behind. At the finish line on the main straightaway, the chief steward and the starter had gotten out the black

Jones roars across the finish at Indy to win the 1963 500.

flag. They were ready to call Jones off the track because his car had become a hazard.

The car's owner, J. C. Agajanian rushed up to the starter's stand and begged them not to do it. The crack in the oil tank was horizontal, he said, and when the oil level dropped below the crack, the leaking would cease.

Agajanian was correct. Suddenly Jones found that his car handled better and he increased his speed. The oil leak stopped, the tire dried off, and he continued on to Victory Lane, winning the 500 by 33 seconds over Clark's Lotus.

Debate about the race raged for months among drivers and officials. On one side were those who claimed Jones should have been pulled off the track. Others felt the stewards had acted correctly. Jones was involved in many arguments, including one with driver Eddie Sachs that resulted in a fist fight between them.

Four years later Jones was in the center of another much-publicized Indianapolis controversy. This time he had the revolutionary car, Andy Granatelli's STP Special, powered by a turbine engine. From its beginning in 1911, the 500 had been a race for cars with internal combustion engines. The turbine represented a radical departure. Many drivers believed that turbine-cars should be barred from the race.

"I always figured Indianapolis was a proving ground for automobiles, not airplanes," A. J. Foyt had said. "That jet car has so much power that we just can't compete against it with normal engines."

Granatelli had secretly begun research on the turbine in 1964. When the car was completed in 1967, he had approached Jones about driving it at Indy. At first Parnelli was hesitant, but following fast test drives at Phoenix Speedway and Indianapolis, he accepted the offer, which was believed to have earned him a flat fee of $100,000.

"Sure, I had my doubts, but then I'd been a piston engine man all my life," Parnelli said. "The first time I looked at the car, I realized it was no freak. A lot of money had been spent on its construction and it was a sanitary car. But I knew nothing about the engine and had to be shown. In a test at Indy, I did 162 miles per hour right away and that convinced me.

"The acceleration was blinding, but I had to sock the gas pedal a couple of seconds before I wanted the power because it had a throttle delay. But when that power came on, it really kicked in, pinning me back in the seat.

Parnelli sits in the controversial turbine car before the 1967 Indy 500.

"Driving the car was a very strange experience because there was no sound from the engine, just a little hum and the "whoosh" of it moving through the air. I could hear the joints in the car crackling, the brake discs making contact and the tires screeching. But I figured it could out-run anything at Indianapolis, although we had no idea about its reliability. The tremendous thrust of the engine placed heavy stress on the drive train. And with no gears to slow the car down, I had to use a lot of brakes. They became quite hot."

During practice the car devoured many sets of gears, making it necessary to build expensive stronger ones. When other drivers complained of the heat waves from the turbine engine, Granatelli had a $4,000 shield built to deflect the heat.

"I had fun at the Speedway because everyone was needling me about the car and many people accused me of driving below top speed in practice," Jones said. "That wasn't true. I had no idea what the car would do. I had to learn to drive it there. Just having the four-wheel drive gave the car tremendous road-holding stability through the corners and I had to adjust to that."

Jones qualified the turbo-car in sixth position at 166.075 miles per hour, behind pole-sitter Mario Andretti, who had a 168.982 mph.

Andretti jumped into the lead through the first turn, but on the short chute leading to the second turn, Jones moved the big red car high to the outside of the track, punched the accelerator and emerged from the second turn in front. The turbine car gradually pulled away from the pack and when the race was halted by rain after 18 laps, Parnelli had a 12-second lead.

On the following day's restart, Jones began to lengthen his lead on the first lap. At the 50-lap mark, his margin over Foyt was 25 seconds. Jones went into a spin to avoid another car on lap 52, and Dan Gurney moved into first place briefly. But Jones quickly caught Gurney and passed him. During the turbo-car's first pit stop A. J. Foyt went ahead, but again Jones caught up quickly.

Soon Parnelli was running consistent laps of 158 mph, rolling along with a 50-second lead on Foyt. When 20 miles remained in the race, his pit crew flashed Jones an "E-Z" sign on the pit board and some members of the crew headed for Victory Lane.

Then, near the end of his 197th lap, a $6 ball

bearing in the gearbox of the turbo-car gave out, depriving the car of all power. The crowd of more than 200,000 spectators groaned as Jones coasted slowly around turn four.

"I was riding along counting the laps to the finish," Jones said. "I could see Foyt ahead of me but almost a lap behind and I figured the old race was all mine. Suddenly there was a loud noise and the car behaved like I'd thrown the gearshift into neutral. I had no idea what had happened. I was numbed by it. I just coasted back to the pits and parked it."

Foyt roared down the straight and into the lead to win his third Indianapolis 500. Parnelli Jones sat in his garage with tears running down his cheeks.

Rufus Parnell Jones was born in Texarkana, Arkansas, in 1933. He grew up in Torrance, California, a tough town near Los Angeles. His family owned a Model A Ford which had a push-pull switch instead of an ignition key. When his father was away from home, he removed the rotor from the engine to prevent young Rufus from driving it.

"I bought a rotor of my own in a junkyard, put it in the car and drove it through the fields," Jones recalled. "When I was 12, I used to climb over the fence at the local hot rod track and watch the races. Troy Ruttman was winning most of the races then and he later won the Indy 500. He was my hero although I had no ideas about being a race driver. Besides, my mother worried about me getting hurt riding my bicycle, so she wouldn't have taken too kindly to any chatter about racing cars.

"I was more interested in horses, anyway. I worked in a riding stable, saved my money and bought a horse. Then I traded it for a hot rod when I was 16 and had my driver's license. I never finished school. I quit at 16 and got a job in a garage because all I was interested in was cars.

"It just sort of happened that I became a race driver. I ran with a wild crowd of kids and we used to buy old crates from the junkyards. We'd take them out in the fields and tear around. We'd roll them over and play chicken. Two of us would run at a wall and the first guy to turn away was the loser, the 'chicken.' I don't know how we avoided serious injuries because we never used seat belts."

Jones began to race competitively at 17, driving jalopies at the local track. A relative had blown the engine in her 1934 Ford and he rebuilt the engine for racing. He towed the car to the local track, blew the engine again in the warmup and towed it home.

"We fixed up the car and went back to the track," Jones said. "About all I had going for me was guts. I ran into other cars and hit walls. I rolled the car over, too, but I'd done that often enough out in the fields with old wrecks so that it didn't scare me much.

"Another kid and I ran an old jalopy Ford in stock car races," Jones said. "He liked to tease me by adding the 'i' to Parnell. He knew I didn't like it because it sounded like 'Nellie,' who was a girl we both hated. One day, he painted 'Parnelli' on the car and the name caught on."

Parnelli soon learned that racing can be expensive. He ran out of money and stayed out of racing for more than a year. He quit his garage job to work for a friend in the cement business, saving his money and building a new jalopy in his spare time. When he returned to the track in 1953, this car carried him to his first victory.

During the next three years, Jones competed in three races a week. He gradually learned to drive within his car's limits and soon began winning consistently. One day a friend who drove in the modified stock car division, the next class above the jalopies, didn't want to drive. Parnelli took his car instead and won the race, earning a chance to compete regularly in the higher level of competition. Soon he was driving regularly for owner Harlan Fike. He started with modified cars, but soon advanced again, this time to the sprint class.

Parnelli was a big winner in the International Motor Contest Association sprint and midget series in the midwestern and eastern United States in 1958 and 1959. He also attracted the interest of car owners Vel Miletich and J. C. Agajanian, two men who were to play an important role in his later career.

In 1960, driving a Chevrolet-powered sprint car, Jones joined the U.S. Auto Club circuit, the top league for sprint machinery. He competed against wise veterans such as Don Branson and Jud Larson and up-and-coming youngsters Jim Hurtubise and A. J. Foyt. The competition was brutal but Jones quickly became a leading contender. He won the Midwest Championship in 1960. Then the USAC initiated a national sprint car championship and Parnelli won the title in 1961, 1962 and 1964.

Even while he was racing on the sprint car circuit,

Jones got his first chance at big-car competition. J. C. Agajanian provided the car for a 1960 100-mile race at Milwaukee, Wisconsin. In 1961 Jones entered the Indianapolis 500 for the first time, qualified fifth fastest and led the race for 27 laps. He finished 12th and was named Rookie of the Year at Indy. He won his first championship event at Phoenix, Arizona, later that year.

In the 1962 Indy race Jones earned the pole position, qualifying with the first 150 mile-per-hour lap

A fierce competitor in any kind of race, Parnelli drives a Mercury Cougar to victory in a 1969 Trans-Am race.

in Speedway history. He led the race for 120 of the first 125 laps. But then his brakes failed and he was forced to slow down. He finished seventh.

During the next half dozen years, Parnelli drove 50 to 60 races annually and estimated that he won "about 150" races in sprint, stock and championship cars. In 1965 he won the rich Riverside, California, sports car race against a strong field of international drivers.

Then in 1966 he reduced his schedule to a few selected races such as Indianapolis and a few big purse stock car events.

"When you're running 50 to 60 races a year, you've got no respect for the speeds you're running," he said. "Sooner or later you reach a point where you better stop and take a look at what you're doing. I reached that point when I hit the wall in a race at Trenton, New Jersey, in 1965. I took a good look at myself and cut back on my driving program."

But when the car was right and the Jones competitive fires burned again, he was a driver to reckon with. He had the talent, the nerves and the spirit of a champion.

10

Bobby and Al Unser

Victory Lane at the Indianapolis Motor Speedway is a small fenced-off area at the end of the pit lane. Each May the winner of the annual 500-mile auto race enters the lane after driving his victory lap. There he is greeted by his ecstatic crew, is kissed by the race queen and is interviewed on the track's public address system.

One of the people most familiar with Victory Lane was not a hardened race driver or an owner of winning cars. Mrs. Mary Unser was a tall, gray-haired woman from Albuquerque, New Mexico, famous in racing circles for her homemade chili and her race-driver sons.

Three times in four years, Mrs. Mary Unser was in Victory Lane to greet her boys following their victories in the world's richest auto race. Bobby Unser won the race in 1968. His brother, known in racing circles as "Baby Al," triumphed in 1970 and 1971. In each of the three years the Unser boys gave their mother a gigantic hug before they kissed the glamorous race queen.

Racing was a way of life to the Unser boys. Their father, two uncles and several cousins had partici-

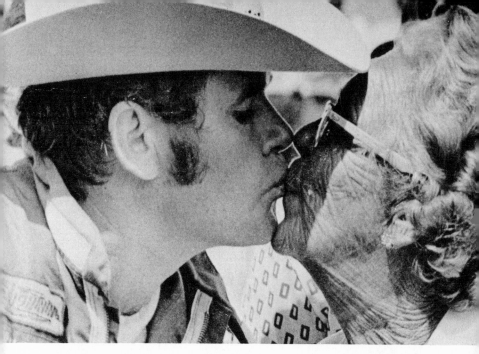

Mrs. Mary Unser gets a kiss from son Al Unser in Victory Lane after Al won the 1971 Indy 500.

pated in the sport. Their brother Jerry was killed at Indianapolis during practice for the 1959 race. Another brother, Louie, had driven and worked as a race mechanic until crippled by muscular dystrophy.

The Unser clan frequently was called "The Royal Family of U.S. Racing," but there were several other candidates for the title. Lee Petty and his son Richard were two of the three men ever to win three national championships in NASCAR stock car racing. Famed Indianapolis driver Tony Bettenhausen was followed into racing by his three sons, Gary, Merle and Tony, Jr. Two-time Indy winner Bill Vukovich established a tradition which his son, Bill, Jr., continued. However, no family produced as many racers as the Unsers of New Mexico.

"There wasn't much hope that Bobby and I

would be anything else but race drivers," Al Unser said. "We grew up in a world of cars and we had no idea of any other careers. When other kids were playing with their wagons and tricycles, we were around racing cars. Bobby and I always have been very close, but on the track we'll compete against each other as hard as we do against the other drivers. I've had some of my toughest races against Bobby, because he's not about to give me an edge in anything at anytime."

"There have been many times when my toughest competition in a race was brother Al," Bobby commented. "It was that way because he's one great race driver. It's funny, but when we're going at it wheel-to-wheel, I forget that he's my brother. He's just another driver on the track who I have to beat to win the race. But deep down inside, we both worry about each other on the track. If something happens to Al's car. I want to know immediately what it is."

The Unsers' pit crews always had an agreement that if.anything happened to either driver's car during a race, the other pit crew would be informed immediately to permit the information to be relayed to the other brother.

An example of this concern came during the 1968 Indianapolis 500. On lap 41, Al's car collided with the wall and was severely damaged. When Bobby drove past his pit on the next lap, his board read, "Al OK." When he approached his brother's wrecked car, Al was standing on the wall beside the car, waving his arms to make certain Bobby could see that he wasn't injured.

"I knew Al's car had smacked the wall and believe me, I was pretty worried during the next lap until I came past the pit and saw the sign," Bobby said. "It was a great relief to see him waving to me."

Outside of their ability to make a race car move quickly, the Unsers were quite different. The eldest by five years, Bobby was tall and gangly with blond hair. He was a quick-witted man and was not hesitant to express his opinions. Al was shorter and had black hair. He was quieter than his brother and more relaxed. In a race car, the differences disappeared. Each was a charger, a strong competitor who wanted to run in front. Al probably was the smoother driver of the two, but Bobby compensated with strength and determination.

While the Unsers became big names on the oval at Indianapolis, their favorite event was the Pikes Peak Hill Climb in Colorado. For many years, the timed run up the steep, twisting 12.5-mile dirt road was included in the U.S. Auto Club championship circuit and the Unser family dominated the event to earn the title "Kings of the Hill."

The Unser brothers' father, uncles and brother had won the climb several times. Bobby won it for the first time in 1956 when he was 22 years old. He won it six consecutive years from 1958 to 1963, and added victories in 1966 and 1968. Al won Pikes Peak in 1964 and 1965, following two second-place finishes to Bobby. Between them, they had won the event eleven times in thirteen years.

"The Unser family had this tradition about Pikes Peak," Bobby said. "The other members of the family had won it so often that when Al and I came along

we just had to maintain the family standard. It was a specialized sort of race and the key to our winning it so often was preparation. We used to spend a lot of time and money building and preparing a car for Pikes Peak and it cost us more than the prize money we earned. But it became a big challenge to continue the Unser tradition."

"I raced in my first hill climb when I was 20 years old and it was a pretty frightening experience because you had to rip around those mountain turns as fast as possible," Al added. "I was second to Bobby twice, which got to be a little tiresome; then I ended his long winning streak in 1964. He was a little sore about it, but I knew he was happy that if he had to get beaten, it was by another Unser."

Bobby Unser had started his racing career in 1949, driving modified stock cars in New Mexico when he was only 15 years old. In 1950 and 1951, he won the modified stock championship of the state, then expanded his racing horizons into midget and sprint cars. His first major victory came in the 1956 Pikes Peak event.

"Those were busy times for me," he said. "I raced in just about any car I could find that was reasonably safe. Of course, having so much racing expertise in my own family was a big help. They passed along all sorts of good advice to me and they also told me about it when I was doing something wrong."

Bobby's heavy schedule in all types of cars gave him a solid background of experience when he made

A car roars up the tortuous route of the Pikes Peak Hill Climb.

his debut in the Indianapolis 500 in 1963. However, he encountered several heart-breaking failures at Indy before he attained success. In 1963 he qualified 16th but spun out of the race on the third lap. In 1964 he was injured in a second-lap accident.

The following year at Indy, Bobby wrecked his top car, a four-wheel drive Novi, in practice when a car spun in front of him. Driving his backup car, he was running fifth in the race when a broken oil fitting put him out after 69 laps.

By 1966 Bobby was a driver to be reckoned with in USAC championship racing. Although he qualified 28th at Indianapolis, he cut through the field to rank ninth after 41 laps. Then a 28-minute pit stop dropped him out of contention. He finished eighth in the national championship standings, however, and was third in the USAC midget series. Another long pit stop chopped down a potential high finish in the 1967 Indianapolis race. He was forced to spend six minutes in the pit and finished ninth. However, he ranked third in the championship standings at the end of the season.

Al Unser's climb up racing's ladder of success included many of the steps taken by his brother. At 18 he was racing modified stockers in Albuquerque. He apprenticed in midget and sprint cars, then made his debut in championship cars in 1964.

Success at Indianapolis and on the championship trail came more quickly to Al than it had to Bobby Unser. Al made his first Indy appearance in 1965 and a steady driving performance earned a ninth-place finish.

Brothers Bobby (above) and Al (below) pose in their cars.

In 1965 he qualified 23rd at Indianapolis and was running in third place on lap 161 when he spun into the wall at the start of the main straightaway. At the time he was 17 seconds in front of eventual winner Graham Hill. Al earned three second-place finishes in championship trail races and was fifth in the point standings at season's end.

In 1967 Al moved into the front ranks of USAC drivers with a second-place finish at Indy and another fifth-place finish in the final championship ranking. He also finished fifth in the USAC stock car division.

Al started his 1968 season in fine fashion by finishing fourth in the Daytona 500 stock car race. Although his Indy attempt ended when he smacked the wall, he won five consecutive championship trail races. Those triumphs plus several other high placings carried him to third in the standings. He won the USAC stock car race at Mosport and was fourth in that series.

"Both Unser boys had an immense desire to succeed that was obvious from the time they started to race championship cars," said one USAC driver. "I think Al had more natural talent than Bobby. Al always was very smooth. However, Bobby was a great competitor and while it took him a little longer than Al to reach the top, his great ambition made up for anything he lacked in natural talent."

The Unser brothers' victories in the Indianapolis 500 were as different as the men themselves.

In 1968 Andy Granatelli entered his STP-Lotus turbine cars in the race for the second time. The previous year, the turbine driven by Parnelli Jones had dropped out of the race only ten miles from victory. Joe Leonard and Graham Hill were the turbine drivers in 1968, and Leonard had smashed the Indy records by qualifying at 171.5 miles per hour. Leonard took the pole position, Hill was second on the grid and Bobby Unser was the third man in the front row in his Eagle, powered by a turbo-charged Offenhauser engine.

Leonard grabbed the lead and Bobby settled into second place. Bobby's Eagle carried a four-speed gearbox instead of the normal two-speed equipment, but the gears fouled early in the race.

"Two of the gears were for getting out of the pits quickly," Unser explained. "The third gear was for running with a full fuel tank and the fourth for when the tank was near empty. Early in the race I had to hold the car in gear with my right hand and drive with one hand. But I got a blister on my palm so I gave it up, let the gearshift jiggle around and drove with two hands."

On lap eight, Bobby passed Leonard on the main straight. He held the lead until he made his third and final pit stop on lap 165. Lloyd Ruby and Leonard moved in front of him. Bobby came slowly out of the pits with only one of his four gears operating correctly. Ruby held the lead for nine laps until his car failed. Now Leonard moved in front, running effortlessly in the silent turbine car, seeming to be on his way to a certain win.

With 19 laps remaining in the race, an accident brought out the yellow caution flag and the field slowed to 120 miles per hour for the next 10 laps. Rules call for the drivers to maintain their position and distance between the cars under the yellow. But Leonard's eight-second lead on Unser was cut to five seconds by some jockeying in the pack. Then Leonard's turbine teammate, Art Pollard, a lap behind but running directly in front of Unser, slowed down, forcing Bobby to do the same. Suddenly Leonard's lead was 15 seconds.

On lap 191, the green flag was waved, the signal to resume racing. The drivers stood on the accelerators. Leonard's car shot ahead briefly, and then the engine died. The big red wedge-shaped car rolled on to the infield as Unser roared into the lead. Leonard's fuel pump drive shaft had broken when he accelerated.

Bobby continued on to Victory Lane where he was greeted by a smiling, proud Mom Unser, his wife and their daughter. He went on to win the USAC national driving championship by eleven points over Mario Andretti.

Al Unser was well motivated for the 1970 Indy 500. A year earlier, he had been scheduled to drive an excellent car. But in early May he fell off a motorcycle in a Speedway garage area and broke his leg. He missed the race.

Unser's 1970 car was a PJ-Colt, powered by a turbo-Ford engine. The car was owned by Parnelli Jones, Indy winner in 1963, and Vel Miletich. George Bignotti, one of racing's finest mechanics, was the crew chief and builder of the car. From the time they arrived at the Speedway in early May, it was evident that 1970 was their year. Unser was able to run laps of 168 miles per hour almost immediately and he earned the pole position at 170.221.

The race was just as smooth for Al Unser as the month had been. He led for 190 of the 200 laps and was never pressed. He won by 32 seconds over Mark Donohue.

"I only had one bad moment when I got a bit sideways trying to get through a three-car crash late in the race," Al said in Victory Lane. "I ran a rather conservative race. I could have run harder if someone had pushed me."

The Indy 500 was one of the ten races won by Al Unser on his way to the 1970 national driving championship. Al finished with 5,130 points and collected a record $494,149 in prize money. Bobby Unser finished second with 2,260 points.

The Jones-Bignotti team had another superb Colt-Ford for Al in the 1971 Indianapolis 500. He qualified fifth at 174.622 mph, after the faster

Al Unser crosses the finish line, winning the 1970 Indy 500.

McLaren cars of Peter Revson, Mark Donohue and Denis Hulme, and Bobby Unser's Eagle. Al didn't attempt to chase the early leaders, Donohue and Revson. He sat just off the pace, driving with the consistency and smoothness that always characterized his work.

As the front-runners dropped out with mechanical problems or fell back, the race shaped into a duel between the Unser boys and Al's teammate, Joe Leonard. The lead changed hands eight times in 50 laps in some brilliant driving until Al Unser assumed command of the race on lap 118 and gradually built a solid lead.

Late in the race, Bobby Unser spun into the wall at turn four, trying to avoid Mike Mosley's car, which had gone out of control after losing a tire. Bobby was stunned momentarily but had no injuries.

Al continued on to win and collected $238,454 in prize money. He was helped in the race by a one-way radio which he used to tell the crew exactly what adjustments were required on pit stops. The crew was at work before the car came to a full stop and Al's short times for stops helped him hold onto the lead.

Following his Indy success, Al encountered mechanical gremlins during the remainder of the championship trail. He finished fourth in the final standings while Bobby was sixth.

In the 1970s the Unsers both ranked in the top five on USAC's all-time point standing list and they were at the peak of their careers. Mrs. Unser seemed likely to have more chances to visit Victory Lane.

Index

Page numbers in italics refer to photographs.

Agajanian, J. C., 125, 127, 133, 134
Alexander, Tyler, 81
Allison, Bobby, 25
American Hot Rod Association (AHRA), 94
Amon, Chris, 71, 82, 102
Andretti, Mario, 15–16, 19, 54, 56–70, 106, 130, 146
  early life, 61–63
  Indianapolis 500, 1969, 56–60
  photographs of, *58, 60, 66, 68*
Ascari, Alberto, 62, 65, 67, 110
Atlanta International Speedway, 23, 25
Auckland University (New Zealand), 78

Beanland, Colin, 79
Belgian Grand Prix, 47, 48, 111, 117
Bettenhausen, Gary, 137
Bettenhausen, Merle, 137
Bettenhausen, Tony, 137
Bettenhausen, Tony, Jr., 137
Bianchi, Lucien, 15

Bignotti, George, 146
Bondurant, Bob, 48
Brabham, Jack, 78, 80, 81, 117
Branson, Don, 133
Brawner, Clint, 57, 63
British Grand Prix, 52, 82
Brooks, Tony, 79
Bucknum, Ronnie, 15–16

Canadian American Challenge Cup (Can-Am), 54, 71–72, 82, 83, 97, 98, 102, 103, 104
Canadian Grand Prix, 38–41, 52, 53, 54, 99
Cantwell, Chuck, 109
Cevert, Francois, 39, 54
Chapman, Colin, 45, 56, 111, 117
Clark, Jim, 22, 41, 45, 51, 54, 64, 82, 110–122, 125, 127
  early life, 116–117
  Indianapolis 500, 1963, 117–119
  photographs of, *112, 115, 118, 122*
Cox, Don, 109

Daytona 24-Hour Race, 102
Daytona 500 Grand National, 33, 144
Dean, Al, 65
Dickson, Larry, 56
Dixie 500 Grand National, 25
Donohue, Mark, 82, 97–109, 147, 148
    early life, 101–102
    Trans American Sedan Championship, 1970, 106–107
    photographs of, *99, 101, 105, 108*
Drag racing described, 85–87
Dutch Grand Prix, 49, 52, 53, 117

Ecurie Ecosse, 43, 44

Fangio, Juan Manuel, 110, 111, 121
Fike, Harlan, 133.
Firecracker 400, 17
Follmer, George, 71, 106
Foster, Billy, 64
Foyt, Anthony Joseph, Jr., 11–24, 59, 65, 120, 130, 133
    early life, 19–20
    Indianapolis 500, 1961, 20–21
    Indianapolis 500, 1964, 22
    Indianapolis 500, 1967, 12–14
    Le Mans Endurance Race, 1967, 15–17
    photographs of, *13, 14, 16, 21, 24*
French Grand Prix, 48, 52, 54

Garlits, Don, 85–96, *88–89, 91*
    early life, 92

German Grand Prix, 49, 52, 54, 79, 112
Granatelli, Andy, 12, 56, 60, 67, 128, 144
Great Britain Grand Prix, 54
Gregory, Masten, 80
Gurney, Dan, 15–16, 102, 130

Hall, Jim, 77, 102
Hamilton, Pete, 35
Hansgen, Walt, 102
Hill, Graham, 46, 48, 49, 50, 66, 111, 113, 117, 122, 145
Hill, Phil, 102
Hoosier 100, 17
Hulme, Denis, 49, 50, 54, 68, 71, 81, 83, 98, 104, 148
Hurtubise, Jim, 133

Ickx, Jackie, 52, 65
Indianapolis 500, 11, 12, 17, 20, 22, 23, 63, 68, 98, 106, 111, 113, 117, 119, 120, 144, 146–148
Indianapolis Motor Speedway, 11, 12, 56, 98, 125, 130, 135, 136
Inmans, Dale, 34–35
Italian Grand Prix, 46, 52, 53, 112, 114

Johnson, Junior, 32
Jones, Rufus Parnell (Parnelli), 13, 20, 22, 64, 69, 106, 107, 119, 123–135, *124, 127, 129, 134,* 146
    drives turbine engine, 128–129
    early life, 131–133
    Indianapolis 500, 1963, 125–127

Kerr, Phil, 84

Larson, Jud, 133
Lehigh University, 100
LeMans 24-Hours of Endurance, 11, 12, 15, 17, 23, 65, 82
Leonard, Joe, 69, 107, 124, 145, 148

McClusky, Roger, 15–16, 59
McDonald, Dave, 22
McIntyre, Bob, 44
McLaren, Bruce, 15–16, 45, 64, 71–84, 98, 102, 104
  designer and builder, 72, 75–77, 80–84
  early life, 77–78
  photographs of, *73, 76, 81, 83*
Marshman, Bobby, 22
Mayer, Ted, 80, 81, 84
Mecom, John, Jr., 46
Mexican Grand Prix, 50, 52, 53
Meyer, Louis, 14
Michigan International Speedway, 99
Miletich, Vel, 124, 133, 146
Mille Miglia, 62
Monaco Grand Prix, 46, 52, 54
Moss, Stirling, 110, 111
Motschenbacher, Lothar, 103

Nassau Trophy Race, 21
National Association of Stock Car Auto Racing, (NASCAR), 17, 25, 34, 37
National Hot Rod Association (NHRA), 88, 92, 94
New Zealand Grand Prix, 79

Panch, Marvin, 23

Parsons, Chuck, 98
Pearson, David, 37
Penske, Roger, 82, 97–104, *101,* 106, 107, 109
Peterson, Ronnie, 40, 99
Petty, Lee, 28, *29,* 37, 137
Petty, Maurice, *29*
Petty, Richard, 25–37, 137
  early life, 28–33
  photographs of, *26, 29, 32–33, 36*
Pikes Peak Hill Climb, 139–141, *140*
Pollard, Art, 146

Regazzoni, Clay, 67
Revson, Peter, 71, 109, 148
Rindt, Jochen, 53
Roberts, Fireball, 32
Rose, Mauri, 14
Ruby, Lloyd, 15, 47, 59, 145
Ruttman, Tony, 131

Salvadori, Roy, 79
Sachs, Eddie, 20, 127
Shaw, Wilbur, 14
Siffert, Jo, 39
South African Grand Prix, 45, 52, 53, 54, 61, 68, 117, 121
Spanish Grand Prix, 52, 53, 54, 67
Sports Car Club of America (SCCA), 100, 101
Stewart, Jackie, 27, 38–55, 66, 69, 99
  early life, 42–43
  Indianapolis 500, 1965, 46–47
  photographs of, *39, 42, 47, 49, 53, 55*
Summernationals, 94
Surtees, John, 68, 98, 102, 120

Tasman (New Zealand) Championship, 121
Times Grand Prix, 100
Trans American Sedan Championship (Trans-Am), 98, 103, 105, 106, 124
Travis, Joe, 92
Trintignant, Maurice, 79
Turner, Curtis, 32
Tyrrell, Ken, 45, 48, 49, *53*, 54, 57

United States Auto Club (USAC), 11, 17, 21, 23, 28, 61, 63, 67, 97, 109, 123, 133, 142, 146
United States Grand Prix, 50, 52, 53, 54, 61, 65, 80
United States Road Racing Championship (USRRC), 98, 102, 103, 104
Unser, Al, 69, 98, 124, 136–148, *137, 143, 147*

Indianapolis 500, 1970, 146–147
Indianapolis 500, 1971, 147–148
start in racing, 142–143
Unser, Bobby, 65, 136–148, *137*
Indianapolis 500, 1968, 144–146
start in racing, 141–142
Unser, Jerry, 137
Unser, Louie, 137
Unser, Mary, 136, *137*

Von Tripps, Wolfgang, 79, 114
Vukovich, Bill, 137
Vukovich, Bill, Jr., 137

Ward, Rodger, 20, 22
Weatherly, Joe, 32
Williams, Carl, 71
Winternationals, 88, 94